THE SOULSWIMMER

By the same author:

A Long Stone's Throw

THE SOULSWIMMER

A Collection of Stories, Verses, and Songs

By

Alphie McCourt

CPW BOOKS
NEW YORK, NEW YORK

Copyright © 2014 Alphie McCourt
Published by
CPW Books
New York, New York
www.alphiemccourt.com

Parts of this book were first published in Ireland
under the title *Heartscald* by
Revival Press
Limerick, Ireland
Managing Editor: Dominic Taylor

Cover Design: Dania Fernandez Fernandez with Joe Tantillo
Book Design: Dania Fernandez Fernandez with Joe Tantillo
Illustrations by Ronan Deevy
Editor: Fiona Clark-Echlin with Brent Robison
Author photo by Lynn McCourt

ISBN: 978-0692279380

Library of Congress Control Number: 2014915749
CPW Books, New York, NY

To Michael Ryan, my lifelong friend.

To my late great friend
Seamus O'Dwyer.

To my teachers:
Education opens a window. Our teachers opened a thousand.
With deep appreciation.

Miss Matthews of Henry Street School
Brother Nevin
Mr Stan Downing
Mr O'Shea
Mr Criostoir O Floinn
Brother Brady
Mr Galvin
Mr Malone
Mr Tom Greene
Mr Tony Bromell
Mr Jack Noonan
Reverend Brother Kealy
All at the Christian Brothers Schools, Sexton Street

Cont

Gentle reader, welcome.

You are about to enter the inner world of Alphie McCourt, but just before you come in Management has asked me to have a word. I can say whatever I like, they said.

So here we are in the vestibule. I envy you. You haven't read this unpredictable collection of stories, songs and poetry yet. It will be a good journey. But first, please have a seat. They have left us some comfortable chairs and look, there's tea for everyone. Alphie must have seen to that.

I first met Alphie McCourt in 2009 when his book *A Long Stone's Throw* came out and he was one of our principal guests at the Woodstock Memoir Festival. Since then he has graced every memoir festival to the point where he is one of its honorary godfathers. I have visited him in his New York City home, the one you will be reading about shortly, the one that used to be on the West Side but is now on the Upper West Side. He hasn't moved, but times and names and fashions change.

I like to observe how no matter what is going on in his apartment Alphie can find a corner of quiet and peace. His elderly laptop is set up on a small desk in the living room just as you enter and he is often there. No majestic mountain landscape out the window to inspire, no study where he can close the door and disappear into his thoughts. Alphie does his writing on the run. You'll find out that wherever his day takes him the writing comes along—on scraps of paper thrust into pockets. Most of that writing survives its unprotected birth, though not all of it.

Of what does Alphie write? What will you find in these pages? You will find the inner workings of a man always on the alert, watching with the eyes of a poet, seeing those in the crowd whom no one else notices, shaking his fist at the well-fed politician who promises more of the same, and always noticing the gold of the onion skin.

I am glad Alphie writes. I would like him so much even if he did not. But because he writes he shares so much more of himself. He lets us in on what preoccupies him as he walks through the Village or stands in a subway car. And it's not always the musings of a sensitive soul. Sometimes you'll get a crazy little story about a farmer banging his wife in a cowshed. You never know what you'll get when you turn the page in Alphie's book.

Ah. I see you have finished your tea. It probably had a little more bite than you expected. Well, I guess you'd best be on your way. I hope you are not in a rush. If you are, then carry the book with you and sample it whenever you can. But I hope you can linger. If one story doesn't grab you, keep going, the next one will be totally different. But no matter what, you will know that it is Alphie McCourt talking to you, Alphie letting you in on the side of himself that so many of us have no idea how to articulate.

Marta Szabo
Authentic Writing
www.authenticwriting.com
Woodstock, NY
August 2014

The

Soulswimmer

Song: *The Soulswimmer*

She's a beautiful illusion, she is real
Brings light and bright fusion makes me feel
Moonbeam to my dreams sunlight in my mind
She can never be confined

Swimmer in my soul
She's the swimmer in my soul

Sometimes she goes away without a trace
In every frame on every wall I see her face
And the waiting heart yearns
For the time when she returns
And brings her smile her elegance her style

Swimmer in my soul
She's the swimmer in my soul

And now I know it's time to say goodbye
She's takin' off for good she even told me why
She's got to make a start
Ease the aching in her heart
To pick up on the challenge in her mind

Swimmer in my soul
She's the swimmer in my soul

She'll go lightly like a dancer
Bound to find the answer
And forever be the swimmer in my soul
The swimmer in my soul.

Social

Prince Harry Done Bin and Gone:
Bring On Our Monarchy

Prince Harry: he came, he saw, he conquered. Men admire him. Women love him. His mother Princess Diana died in a car accident in Paris in 1998. In our friends' house, in Pennsylvania, we learned that she had been badly injured and, later, that she was dead. I was sad. My wife was deeply disturbed. She continued to watch the television coverage of the tragedy. I went on up to bed.

When I came down in the morning she was already transfixed by the news footage. Diana was stylish and glamorous, her good works praiseworthy. I was deeply saddened, especially because of her youth and beauty, but I felt no connection.

I tried to articulate all this but my brain was still sleeping. "Oh, is she still dead?" was what came out of my mouth. In an awkward moment I had uttered a stupid and seemingly callous remark. It was not what I meant to say. Some months later I asked Lynn why women feel so strongly about Diana. "Women have few heroes," she said. "Diana was superstar, superhero, and an English princess."

Let's face it: We have "a thing" for the English. We admire them and condescend to them in equal measure. We are also intimidated by them. Public Television depends heavily on British programming. During the 1970s the long running series Upstairs, Downstairs fed our fascination with the English upper classes and their servants. Downton Abbey is our latest craze. Set on a large estate, it has an English lord and his American wife, as central characters. The English are forever fascinated by the First World War. And with good reason. Downton begins before the outbreak of that war, continues on through and chronicles the changes that took place in English society after the war. We are no less fascinated.

The English yearn for the days when everyone in England was English, when people knew their place, when honor prevailed, and order. Who would begrudge our own yearning for a dash of nobility and honor, of style, even? Blue and red, absolutists all, we are stuck between lockstep liberals and fevered fundamentalists. Is it any wonder that we look to the Downton Abbey of another time for order, stability and clarity?

Good old- fashioned openness in government has given way to something called transparency. Our leaders travel in bulletproof vehicles with tinted windows, all in the interest of security, we are assured. There is no access to our leaders. "Money makes women horny," Willie Nelson once said, a quote he attributed to Ray Price. It takes a king's ransom to run for office and payback is a you-know-what. And so, money also buys access.

What can we do? Well, we could burnish the illusion that ours is a fair system with liberty and justice for all. But why bother, when we have a de facto aristocracy already in place and the poor are relearning their proper place, while the shrinking middleclass juggles the mortgage for all. And we are blessed with a virtual guarantee of perpetual war, "over there," our no-fault insurance against ever having to bear responsibility for the bottomless chasm at home.

We can bow our heads in tribute to the Founding Fathers and still ensure that privilege takes precedence. But it's all so dull and temptation is great. We're human, after all and, as Oscar Wilde said, the best way to get rid of a temptation is to yield to it.

So why not kill two stones with one bird, keep our simulacrum of democracy—and get us a monarch to top it off? You can lease a car, a jet, or rent an escort. Why not a king or a queen? Our monarch should be English. An English-speaking king or queen will cement "the special relationship." As a rental, the monarch's status will not violate the constitution and, since he or she is only a temp, we will not have to pay retirement or other benefits.

Surely we can find a Royal cousin willing to take the job. (Harry would be terrific but a Royal, wearing two crowns, would raise constitutional issues). The monarch's term of office would run for no more than eight years, concurrent with the term limits imposed on the president. Lend-lease worked well during the War. Rent-A-Royal should work equally well. We gain a cornerstone for our new and improved democracy: Britain saves a ton of money on the upkeep of one Royal.

To distinguish ours from the British monarch, HRH, Her Royal Highness, our King/Queen will be dubbed His/Her Royal Rented Highness: HRRH. HRRH will spend two thirds of the year in the royal castles in Disney World and Disneyland. The remaining few months will be spent traveling to Minnesota, for the ice fishing, or to New York, for the shopping, as the case may be. The Department of Royal Maintenance will administer the royal affairs.

HRRH will never appear in Congress, though he or she may ring the opening bell at the New York Stock Exchange, upon request. Monarch and consort will dress in ceremonial attire a few times a year. Politicians, power brokers, and their consorts will join them and dress accordingly. Once a year HRRH will dine at the White House. Horse and carriage will be the mode of transportation on these occasions.

Soon the leaders of the blue and red parties will forswear their divisive ways and readily appropriate a ton of money to maintain the royal establishments. The rich will grow richer, the privileged more privileged, and the poor even more impoverished. Our stars will be perfectly aligned.

And what of the citizen? The citizen will keep his head down. Days, nights, and weekends he will toil, multi-tasking, doing three jobs, thankful to be paid for one. Distracted by foreign wars and royal spectacle at home he will appear not to notice his enslavement to ever longer working hours. And the disappearance of his children's opportunities into the maw of the Twenty-First Century.

The monarch, meanwhile, will attend the Super Bowl, with retinue in tow. Or imagine HRRH at the Kentucky Derby, knee-deep in old money and fawned upon by the chosen. The Yeas and Nays of democracy will soon be drowned out by the Oohs and Aahs of our royalist fantasies.

HRRH will captivate the men and wow the women. In our indifference to the corruption of our democratic tradition we will be united. Political discourse will die and dissent become but a distant memory.

What now of the citizen? The citizen has been silent, yes, but he is never indifferent. Weary, now, of frippery, and sick and tired of war, he will soon rise up at the ballot box. Vote N.O.T.A., vote None Of The Above, (or Throw The Bums Out), will be his battle cry. Then, with regret, (for the monarch is a good guy and a Dodgers fan), he will fire the Royal. (With a year's notice, a good reference and, of course, a decent severance package). And we will start afresh.

Fundamentalist Cyclists Have Me Praying for Relief

In the mid-1970s I lived in San Francisco and worked in a restaurant in Marin County, across the Golden Gate Bridge, 14 miles from the city. I rode the bus. Sometimes, when I worked late and the buses had stopped running, I caught a ride to the freeway and hitchhiked from there.

One night I caught a ride in a van. The driver and I were roughly the same age, about 35. He addressed me as "sir." Two longhairs, we talked a bit, mostly about where we were from and how we grew up. He continued to call me "sir."

Across the Golden Gate we went and on into the city. He drove me to the building where I lived, down behind the Opera House, on a street full of whores. He had mentioned "the club" a few times. Now, as I alighted from the van, again he mentioned "the club."

"The club?" I said. "What's the club?"

"The Hells Angels," he said. "Oh," said I.

This Angel-biker had gone out of his way for me. Would a New York City cyclist do likewise? Perhaps, but cyclists tend to be more elitist than bikers. Leather jackets, beards, boots, and booze are not for them.

Two years ago, as I walked by the Church of the Holy Apostles, on Ninth Avenue and 26th Street, I was reminded of this. On that day, the people, mostly homeless men, were waiting outside the soup kitchen. A small knot of men had spilled over from the sidewalk and into the bike lane, where an official person with a clipboard did his headcount, or whatever business he was conducting.

I would have to make my way through the small crowd. Out of the knot of people came a cyclist in all his finery. He had had to slow down and he was annoyed, outraged, even. He passed me, too close for comfort, and his shirt sleeve brushed against mine.

I am up in years, a lifelong pedestrian and subway rider. Once or twice a week I must drive in Manhattan. Now, if I were driving with the window rolled down, and my sleeve happened to touch the sleeve of a cyclist, what would happen? There would be the spit of outrage, the lawsuit, the settlement, and a rise in my insurance premiums.

Last year, on Eighth Avenue, I was standing in the street, in the parking lane, just south of the crosswalk, when a car reversed into me. It was a heavy impact but, luckily, the car suffered no damage. Nor did I. The driver emerged briefly, sat back in, resumed his reverse all the way across the crosswalk, and achieved his parking spot. That parking lane is now a bike lane. When it comes to bike lanes, we pedestrians know to look both ways. I should have known it then.

Self-appointed and -anointed, cyclists perceive themselves as centurions of the climate. There is a whiff of fundamentalism about the mayor's approach and in the attitude of these pedaling apostles of the environment. Fundamentalism, at its best, and there is no best, is a prayer before dying. At its worst, and there sure is a worst, it's a prayer before killing. We need the separation of Bike and State.

I grew up on a bicycle. To a boy on a bike, open road with no traffic in sight—that's freedom, pure freedom, as close as I would ever come to flying. When I was 15, a small group of us rode the 80 miles, over the Kerry Mountains, from Limerick to Killarney. We carried blankets, ground sheets, tents, pegs, and food for the weekend. On Saturday night we cooked and camped out. On Sunday the rains came. We were experienced campers. Even so, our stuff still got soaked. On Monday, with double the weight, we rode back to Limerick. That was our Tour de Kerry.

And once, on a beautiful New York Sunday, on rented bikes, a friend and I rode downtown from the East 70s to the Staten Island Ferry, halfway round the island, back to the ferry and back uptown. That was a great day.

I wish I could tell all this to the cyclist who's having a hissy breakdown because a foolish pedestrian stepped in front of him or because some driver avoided him, only at the last minute, as he angled around the offside of the car. Would he listen? Or would he rather have his hissy?

There's nothing holy about riding a bicycle. No reverence is due. The bicycle may become a good and efficient way to travel around the city but there is little freedom in it. I can't imagine how anyone could enjoy riding in city traffic. Unless she's towing an agenda. Or can it be the challenge? New York is renowned as a walking city. True, you have to be prepared for the taxi breaking the red light, the car cutting it too close, the garbage truck going beep-beep-beep as he backs up. But we're used to it.

Courtesy and deference should be characteristic of the new apostles of the environment. Not so, in my experience. Instead, there is a petulant insistence on their rights, with little or no regard for their own duty of care. That will have to change, now. It will take cooperation, an approach that eschews elitism, fundamentalism, and the cult. The city belongs to all of us.

It belongs to the weekday bicycle messengers, stripped down and built for speed, the bag of top-secret financial documents slung over the shoulder, bike-dancing through clustered pedestrians and traffic jams. There's a lightness, a symmetry, in their perfectly engineered approach. And it belongs to the restaurant deliverymen, too often scorned as illegal immigrants, as they trundle along on heavier bikes. I defend them. They are working. More important, I have never been hit by one. Come rain, come snow, I marvel at the determination of these disciples of the pizza. Where would we be without them?

Now, with bicycle rental stations offering convenient pickup and drop-off locations, even I will be tempted. Some years ago it was reported that a starlet had "accessorized" with a puppy in her handbag. (What's next? An infant?) How about a puppy-rental station to go with the bikes and she can accessorize to her heart's content.

Some years ago, at a charity breakfast, I was asked to introduce the author of a book on schizophrenia among the Irish.

"There is no humor in mental illness," I began. And I stopped. The audience laughed—the uncertain laugh of relief. The truth is there may well be more humor in mental illness than there is in the subject of bike lanes. Yes, let's save the environment, but, in our zealotry, let's not forget to show a degree of consideration for the person standing next to us.

The licensing and registration of bicycles is inevitable, along with special rules for the puppy on the crossbar. And traffic tickets, for a new "revenue stream." Drivers, riders and pedestrians will form a new coalition against this additional imposition. Neighborhood groups and community boards will do their job. Hysteria will die down and the city will move on to the next.

Song For a Disappointed Woman

Bustlin' time on a New York City street
People rushin' on by their eyes don't ever meet
Hustlin' on home now to family and friends
With relief and expectation, at workin' day's end

Now there she goes so serious this forty-somethin' beauty
Carefree days all gone now begins her life of duty
Disappointed woman facing down the downing days
Busy now just keepin' up with this world's changin' ways

She could have done it different, maybe would have had a child
But the man she loved was married even married he was wild
Man she loved was married, even married he was wild

It was easy in her twenties when life was warm and bright
She's facing now a different road has trouble seeing the light
In self defense her look says stay …please stay away
She fears it and resents it the fading of the day

She could have done it different maybe would have had a child
But the man she loved was married even married he was wild
Man she loved was married even married he was wild

But then at a smile from a frolicking child
Her face again shows beautiful serene and oh so mild
When a man passes by with keen admiring glance
Her lovely eyes remember to sparkle and to dance
Her lovely eyes remember to sparkle…
And… to… dance

Windwolf

Icy city wind, tattered, wilding
Trapped in the sounding chamber
Between outer and vestibule doors,
Mourns its own captivity
With a North Woods urban chorus.

On wind's serrated edge
Spectral wolves sing.
Civilization falters.

The Lynching Tree

But one was innocent, yet hanged
Too bad, he had to pay,
To correct, to deter,
To warn the rest of his ilk,
To warn those left behind.

Trials once were private,
Executions open for all to see;
Trials now are circus,
Injections lethal and very private.

Comes this man most monstrously accused
On trial forever and found, by his peers,
Not guilty, not beyond a reasonable doubt.

Racism of every color,
Money, celebrity and privilege,
All took a hand.
Misuse of office showed up on the stand,
Centuries of savagery hang over our head:
Sprits raped, bodies chopped, hanged, torched
Scream by the evil light of the burning cross.

The man is freed to raise his children motherless,
To grapple the memory of the dead.
It may be over now: done it will never be.
We remain, he and we
To harvest our share
Of the hideous fruit
Of the lynching tree.

Preach Us a Murder

(From the Time of O. J. Simpson)

Saturday on the radio
'Heard It Through the Grapevine'
Again and again, so it seemed,
The weekend of 'The Juice'
And remembered Marvin Gaye
Buried in a neat package of domestic violence.

O. J., how could he
Hand us such a tragedy?
Ah yes, domestic violence again, all so simple!
But still did we not raise him up to transcend race,
As we did the literate, educated Nat Turner
Who, soon enough , himself raised up to pillage with the blade.

And still, we cried: O. J., did he? How could he?
As if we, not he and not his victims, were most pained,
When all the time we knew, deep down, we knew
How could he.

Is he, was he ever one of us?
Or must he wait another hundred years?
Is anyone really one of us?
And anyway, who the hell is us?

Does he live only on sufferance, the athlete, the man?
Made super in somebody's image,
Another fool with a briefcase,
And nothing in it but his soul?

Stretched

(After September 11th)

Yesterday, united in disgust,
We turned from him, retreated, clustered:
Backing away from this castoff,
This accusation barely human barely fit to remind us,
There but for the grace.

There was one on every subway train it seemed
Asleep and stretched across a raft of seats
Awash in yellow dreams,
And bathed in the smells of a martyred life.

Was it only yesterday?
Burned by the terror now
Our disgust, if not entirely banished
And gone, along with the fallen towers
Is tempered, by tragedy, into mild dismay.
And the sleeper is no threat.

Move Along Please
(After September 11th)

Street corner poets proffer
Sheets of rain to the unwashed
Sparse are the words, spare is the frame
Downtown.

Deep is the pit
Deep enough for the never found
And for twenty million Soviets (or was it forty?)
Dead in World War Two,
With room for our city's homeless children,
All thirteen thousand,
Scarcely sheltered and still hungry every night.

"Spectacle is all: sensation rules," I said,
"The little screen devours our past
And steals our future:
Gravitas is dead.
And tragedy mere backdrop to performance."

"Move along," said the man. "That's enough.
This is a no wallowing zone:
If you want to stop the zealot,
Then teach his lackeys how to laugh.
With laughter mock the zeal of the fundamentalist.

Now doff your hat to the memory of the dead:
Salute and then move on.
Smile with your heart, laugh out loud
And always, at all preachings, look askance."

Promise of the Leaves
(After September 11th)

Today, the leaves fall.
Last week, last year, or was it yesterday, the towers
Taking, in their thousands, our sisters and our brothers,
All tumbled into crush and burn
To ache, forever, in the shifting gravel pit of memory.

Leaves fall.
Some are speckled yellow, the few, vestigial, still green.
Russet rules, dark ruby bridge between Summer and Fall.
Just as the red sun, at setting, conjoins the darkness and the light.

For the missing, death is presumed: there's no one to be buried.
Mourning will be forever, forever without limit.

Wonder is that the leaves don't flee.
Massing up to plaster closed the sky
To shield, from sun and light the shame,
The face of man, disgraced before the gods
The gods of anybody's race or faith.

But falling leaves won't fly.
Their nature, patient, is to nourish and forgive
While the sun still slants his long farewell,
Sailing into Winter's pledge,
That yes, oh yes, the promised Spring will come.

Future

Have we ventured all to create latchkey children
Single parent homes and homeless single parents?
Is upward mobility as a national aspiration
But transcendent grasping in translation?
Politicians come and go,
Bullriders in the rodeo.
Greed is in again.
Is this the wave of the future, they asked?
More likely, said he, 'twas foretold in the past.

Over There Over Here

For her baby she begged just a spoonful, that day:
All were starving, too weak, their dead for to bury.

Over here, being late, and in a great hurry:
To my grief I was served up a just-warm latte.

Creed

Song: The Mercury Pool

Sun dips slow and easy right into the mercury pool
Night-time comes on quiet, quiet as can be
Moon comes out all over, swallows all the shadows and the dark
Landscape now for the first time is revealed
You said you would stand by me and never bring me sorrow
Rain, shine, flood, drought we'd go hand in hand
Now your song is changing your voice is not so certain
And I begin to wonder if you care

Fool that I was, fool that I am, fool that I always will be

One foot planted firmly on a thin strip of dry land
The other slipping sliding on the verge of quicksand
Holding on to the scraps of what you call your affection
Knowin' I'm stone crazy knowin' I can't change

Fool that I was, fool that I am, fool that I always will be

Live and learn and learn to love says the wise man in the choir
Deaf man he sits silent ponders pain he's never heard
Blind man listens only for dust motes in the air
Till the man who's never spoken sings again
Song he sings is raw and raspy, flinty, high and lonesome
Words he sings are words nobody ever wants to hear
True, nobody promised, nobody ever told you
That Life and Love would ever treat you fair

Fool that you were, fool that you are, fool that you always will be

Still every day the sun comes back churnin' up by mornin'
Every day a fresh new world comes spinnin' round again, again, again,
again, again
Noontime warms the spirit, the blues take a warnin'
And once again I start to hope like another babe a-bornin'
Once again I start to hope like another babe a-bornin'

The Mouse Before Christmas

"The Christmas tree should last well into the New Year. Don't buy it too early. It will only dry out and shed and shred all over the place. And a dried out tree is a fire hazard." Every Christmas I said it. "The price goes down the closer you get to Christmas." That was my reasoning, a rationale, a rearguard action designed to justify procrastination. I would do just about anything to delay the actual moment of setting out to buy the Christmas tree.

Every year, within my self imposed limit, a radius of ten blocks of our apartment, I bought an eight or nine foot tree and carried it home through the streets of what had become the Upper West Side. This was my ritual, begun in 1974. Now, twenty years later, it is Christmas Eve again and I've secured a nice sized tree. We've rummaged in the back room and unearthed the stand. The tree stands in the northwest corner of the living room. A few strands of lights and my job is done.

Lynn, my wife, has been waiting. There had been little or no Christmas in her Jewish upbringing but she makes up for it. Chanukah, Passover and the principal Jewish holidays, all of these we observe. Easter, Christmas and everyone's birthday, all are cause for celebration. So, on this Christmas Eve, presents are wrapped and ready and she places them under the tree. Lynn and her mother settle themselves on the couch to watch TV and savour the tree.

I retire to the quiet of the kitchen, to a cup of tea, and the newspaper. Kitchen counter, sinks and stove top are loaded with the ingredients for tomorrow's Christmas feast. Dinner tonight is every man for himself. I settle for a pre-Christmas bagel. For ten minutes all is quiet. Then, from the living room, comes a shriek. 'Lynn', I think. 'Something furry on the television. And not for the first time. She'll have changed the channel by now.' I was wrong. Another shriek is follows. Then:
"Alphie, Alphie!"

A rustling among the wrapped presents had captured Lynn's attention. From a sitting position she had leaped over her mother's outstretched legs and taken refuge in the doorway of the apartment.

"There's a mouse, a mouse!" she cries. "Do something! Do something!"

"Do what?" I say.

"Catch him!"

"He's gone, by now," I assure her.

All I want is to get back to the tea, the Christmas bagel and the paper. My wife trusts me and trusts my calm assurance that the mouse is gone. But she doesn't entirely trust me. Experience has taught her to mistrust my fondness for the tea and the bagel. And well she knows my addiction to reading and that when I am reading, I can be oblivious.

"Go and get Tony!" Lynn says.

"I will not," I say. Tony, the building superintendent, is Dominican.

"Dominicans celebrate Christmas on Christmas Eve. He's having a party. I'm not going to disturb Tony. It wouldn't be fair. Why don't you go and talk to him. And ask him for a few glue traps while you're at it. He'll be sympathetic to you. He may even forgive you for disturbing him."

Lynn agrees to go. Anything to escape the monster under the tree. In a few minutes she is back, glue traps in hand.

"Tony wishes you happy hunting and a Merry Christmas."

I say nothing. I place the traps strategically; under the tree, beside the couch, close by the radiator. Then I have an idea; THE CAT! I rouse our China from her turkey dreams, carry her into the living room and place her on the rug. China stretches, yawns and rolls over. 'Useless,' I think. It dawns on me then that this Christmas Eve tree is so fresh and its scent so strong that not even China, a Pennsylvania import, almost a wild cat, can sniff out the mouse.

Lynn and her mother return to the couch. I go back to the kitchen. Tea is finished. The bagel is well on its way to digestion and the newspaper opened to the editorial pages. This is the meat of the newspaper, with text galore, glorious text, and no need to turn any pages for a while. Peace reigns, hand in hand with progress. Again comes a shriek. This time I hurry to the living room. Lynn is already at the elevator. Her mother stands in the doorway.

I look around the living room. Yes, there is a mouse, by the radiator, stuck, now, on a glue trap. China, the huntress, shares the glue trap with the mouse. Her paw is stuck on it. 'There's a lesson here somewhere,' I think, something about the shortage of living space in the city, something about sublets. But I have no time to ponder the question. Mouse and cat are in distress. My wife is leaving me. It will be difficult to explain my wife's departure, on Christmas Eve, no less, especially when I have to name a mouse as co-respondent.

I consider the problem. "Gravitas, not grab ass," I had been told when I was young. "Women respect gravitas. They may not love it. And it doesn't have much sex appeal. They may not even recognize it, but in time of crisis they will respect it." Had I been wearing a hat I would have removed it, scratched my head and placed the hat back on my head. As it was, I just scratched my head, surveyed the situation and walked around the battlefield.

It becomes clear that another pair of hands is called for. But I am alone. Tony, the superintendent, is entitled to a peaceful Christmas Eve. And I can't call upon neighbours, family or friends. How can I remove the cat from the trap without encountering the mouse? How to deal with the mouse without rousing the cat? 'Gravitas, man,' I remind myself.

I hoist China with my left hand, at the same time balancing mouse and glue trap with my right. We three begin a slow march to the bathroom. A stream of lukewarm water in the hand basin soon frees China's paw. She wanders off, stops, licks her paw and continues on.

With the aid of a basin of water I soon free the mouse from the pain of his captivity and place him, glue pad and all, in a paper bag. Gently I slide him over the wall of the park across the street. There he will be at one with his brothers and sisters. Reborn, he will rejoin the Cycle of Life.

Lynn returns to the kitchen and continues her preparations for the Christmas dinner. Nowadays she laughs when we talk about that evening. As for me, every December I remember Christmas Eve and the mouse. With a great fondness I remember him, the mouse who came before Christmas.

Heartscald

Homeless, hungry, handmedowned,
Hawking heavensent havenotness:
Handlettered "Help" hoping.
Haves, homewardbound,
Hearken, hasten, heartrended
Unsee, Unhear, Unknow

A Moment

On river's lip the brave boat angles
soon to plummet to the falls

A hunter hears a distant high note
keening and, abruptly, gone

Somewhere, a child stops crying,
gasps and gathers a long encore

Hatless, now, in the fogged up plate glass
she looks and worries her shining hair
Then turns, with fond anticipation:
he's always loved her in the rain

Now, in breathless expectation,
the lovers teeter at the brink:
Hold, then thrust and counter-thrust
cascading into ecstasy

Ferlinghetti in the Morning

Ferlinghetti before noon
safe haven or precarious perch?
With the gone world
even in its goneness
Gone awry

When less and less in this our age
Is truly seen or heard or felt
Impressions, only, linger, on video or sound
against some wistful future day
Of sepia slotted in allotted time

Then may we begin to grasp
All that has passed us by:

Not so Geoffrey, my friend, for he began with nine,
Pushed on to eighteen,
Then twenty-seven, holes

Of golf and when I hinted that the women waiting
Overheated, impatient, and saddled with the children
must surely give us hell

"Ah yes," he said, "they surely will.
But we'll have had the golf."

Colors

Sound reason, heavy in its dark tones, rarely
bows before bright-hued happiness
Common sense, ever dreadful in its dullness
and by its very nature
Must trample inspiration, heedless.

And yet the gods must surely smile, sometimes,
at a touch of brilliant green,
A dazzling stroke of blue, shining through,
a slice-of-heaven phrase, a hint
Of what might be, if we,
just once would look, would see.

Spring

One step from oblivion, adrift,
Man ponders mortality.
Suddenly sing the birds
While children merrychatter
Homing after school.
Now gleams a bright oasis of promise.

Freedom

Feed our children, teach 'em
And make sure they all have shoes,
Then we're free, to go and save the world.

Raison d'Etre

Lacking an absolute d'etre raison
Each decides just to carry on,
For one it's the fear of his own demise
A shroud the wrong shade,
Casket wrong size,
For another the lack, on the other side
Of sushi, guacamole, or tomatoes sundried.

They say over there they have mineral water to burn
But we're in no hurry to take our turn
For many, though not all
The greatest worry and the greatest pall,
Is the fear of a service, memorial
The disgrace of a gathering really small.

But the concern most serious and overbearing
Is that our laser printers we won't be hearing,
Of PC denied and totally faxless,
And to our mobile apps be forbidden all access.

Rights

Of duty I have none
And when all is said and done
My rights rise above
The law and Constitution.

No matter what I do
(wish that I could say the same for you)
When push comes to shove
I'll get forgiveness, even absolution.

Generations

The old man monumental
With his old pipe sacramental
In answer to my query
Said, "Life would be mighty dreary
Without whiskey and tobacco
(Abstentionists can be a little wacko)

So keep your faddy diets and all your cache
Of good times I've had my ration
And there's neither heat nor passion
In an ice cold Perrier."

Bernice

"I was pushing forty," he confided. "You know how it is. You begin to wonder if anything is worthwhile. Happily married you are and to a great woman. Your five children are all in place and doing well. Your wife runs a warm and efficient household. She has blossomed into a beautiful woman, blossomed a bit too much, perhaps, but she is, still, an admirable woman. Prosperous I was and prosperous I would always remain thanks to my father's foresight in managing the family financial affairs. I was prudent by nature but even if I had not been, the family fortune was festooned with parachutes designed to prevent any precipitous collapse, indeed any collapse whatsoever. And my health has always been good. Still I suffered from a great discontent.

"Afternoons were bad. The malaise often came over me in the afternoon. You were all at school and your mother was on her cream bun run, visiting the sick or engaged in one of her charitable causes. Even the servants fell into a quietude in the afternoon. My eyes were tired from reading. The radio offered nothing to distract me. And it was raining outside, as usual. Not wishing to disturb the servants and my own delicious, if melancholy, solitude, I walked toward the kitchen in the rear of the house, in search of a cup of tea.

"On my way to the kitchen I passed the scullery and the adjoining laundry room. A few stray pieces of clothing lay on the floor. I picked them up, damp and still warm from the wash. I followed the trail into the laundry room. Bernice, Mrs. Holland, was sitting in a chair at the long deal table, gazing into space. Her eyes moist, mouth slightly open, she turned her gaze upon me. We were companions in melancholy. "Bernice" I whispered. "Alistair" she answered. With my fingertips I touched her under the chin and raised her to her feet. Outside, the gentle drizzle had turned into a heavy downpour, an almost tropical rain, beating against the windows of the laundry room.

"A mouse squeaked and ran over Bernice's foot. She screamed, then threw her arms around me, legs around my middle, her face buried in my neck. For a long moment I held her, then sat her on the deal table. She lifted her sweater over her head. The maids were supposed to do the laundry. Why was Bernice in the laundry room? Through her white blouse her nipples were plain to be seen. Now I understood. Bernice's underwear was in the wash. What could I do?" he said. I made no comment. The whole notion of him looking at nipples was ridiculous. And Mrs. Holland's at that. But I was curious. I wanted him to continue with his story. It was better than listening to him talking about his lumbago.

"She was a fulsome woman," Father said, "full in breast and hip but surprisingly long legged. All her years of being starched, stiff and formal fell away before the hammering of the rain, the steamed up windows and our delicious closeness. We tasted each other, oh yes, we damn near devoured each other, secure in the knowledge that no one would arrive home in such weather. And the rest of the staff could be counted upon not to stir on that kind of a day. Bernice assured me that she had always turned a blind eye to their rainy day siestas.

"Later, we lay back on the table. Soon Bernice started to chuckle. 'What is it?' I asked her. 'It's perfect,' she said. 'I was feeling low and lonely. I heard you prowling around the house so I dropped a few pieces of laundry just to bring you my way.' 'You're the devil,' I said. 'And you love it,' she purred.

"In the end she had the best of me. And I let her. She had me on my back on that deal table. With the windows well steamed, tenderness gave way to fire, to triumph, and then to a look of pure love, as she bore down and I gave a final thrust upward and into her. Enmeshed in each other, we cried out together. It was natural. She was a country girl, after all.

"We disengaged, got dressed and kissed; a long, lingering, affectionate kiss. There would be no repeat performance. We knew that. Any attempt to recreate that afternoon would only destroy the memory of it. Neither of us would jeopardize the position of the other. This was love of a different order."

Boots

On the platform,
half-dreaming an early train
We are clattered awake by her wooden heels; dahrrunk, dahrrunk,
dahrrunk

Boots:
On the border,
keeping out the needy,
Stemming the desperate tide of those who cannot survive at home

Boots:
On the ground,
our greatest bugaboo: why boots?
When drones make splendid killers and don't come legless home in
empty boots

Boots:
On the hotel bed,
stiletto heels in combat mode, gouging the Candidate's naked back,
Imploring, "harder, honey, harder: to war, to war, oh yes oh take me all
the way,
Home!"

Song: *The Mall Warriors*

From the malls of Petaluma to the stores of Miami,
We will buy old China's cheapest goods, gifts for you and more for me.
Stagflation grips the nation since the time of Bernanke
We are told to spend as much as we can so the US will stay free

We will go out to the parking lot in the trunk we'll stow our stuff
And if anyone even looks at us we'll sneer to show we're tough.
We've been hangin' here since we were teens, Security knows us well
Still, if we should see a suspicious looking man—we will surely run like hell.

We savor our sliders and our cokes and we love our iced latte,
Show contempt for anyone who smokes and wish they'd go away.
We are fine upstanding citizens; we always know our rights
And we thank our troops for their service, coming legless from the fight.

The rich and powerful don't send their kids so why should we send ours
When there's lots of poor kids ready to go as they try to become
        empowered:
Their efforts we will always cheer and honor them when they're dead
But none of this is really our fight so we'll stay at home—in bed

Mission Statement

Children die of malnutrition
But, dear sir, that's not my mission.
The business that I do, they say,
Will benefit each one,
Some day.

Postpubescent

Postpubescent gazes, unbelieving, unblinking,
At the detritus of the previous generation:
For all their working, striving, surviving, unthinking,
Thinks who the hell is running this nation?

Identity

Look at me, me, me
I have no time for work or play
I am busy night and day
Asserting and preserving my racial, ethnic and sexual identity.

A Conservative's Prayer

Lord, Lord hear my prayer
I don't want to be City Councillor
Or even Mayor,
Please, please and I know you can
Let me continue, ahem,
As always one of us
And never one of them.

Peace by Edict

(From the time of the Texan)

Let Buddha bow to Ramadan
And Christians turn to Buddha
Let Jews shake hands with Islam by damn
Let all love one anudda
And let all eat beef and shellfish and ham
Or we'll nuke ya wid a Scudda.

Potentate
(From the time of the Texan)

Japanese Prime Minister came West
Said to George, "I wish you the best,
Good luck with your next election."
But, given his Asian inflection
George thought that he'd said "erection"
Said, "To hell with him and goddam
Ah'll show them all
Ah'll bomb Saddam!"

To War

To war, to war!
Throw out the rational
Bring on the rationale.

Mad Bull

And then for the first time in oh so many years
With Congressional Republicans expressing their fears
The US was pushing hard for a Northern Ireland Peace
And John Bull came down with Mad Cow Disease.

Polizza

The hoopla was just about over,
The nominee almost in,
(The City's coffers were cascading over,
With our streets, for a week, free of poverty and sin)
When a dutiful policeman
Much relieved, now, and speeding on his own two feet,
Brought four pizza pies to party on the tailgate of a van,
As Clinton's acceptance speech ended and his real work began
At twilight time, by FIT, on Twenty-Seventh Street.

Woman

So beautiful she'd keep an Englishman from washing his car
Make him turn away from the telly
Make a Paddy forgo a trip to the bar
And a middle-aged man suck in on his belly.

Class

The poor and the rich
Are united, though apart,
In their readiness
To admit to a fart.

The others, alas,
The middle class
Will only admit
To passing gas.

Frog

When Frog, a leader of his nation
Forsook his hop and started to jog,
'Twas time to put a stop
To the march of civilization.

The Dove

When a soldier, barely shod and poorly fed,
Shares his scarce ration and saves from near-dead the child,
maybe,
Of his ancient enemy:
Then, surely, the dove will descend.

A Savage Is It?

In 1966 I finished my two years of service in the U.S. Army. A year later, in 1967, I took my G.I. Bill benefit and returned to Ireland to study at University College, Dublin, with the idea of becoming a barrister. The G.I. Bill paid me $130 a month and I supplemented my income by returning to New York, during summer and Christmas vacations, to work in a restaurant.

University College, Dublin, situated in Earlsfort Terrace, off Leeson Street, was on the South Side of Dublin. Dublin's South Side, separated from the unruly North Side by the River Liffey, was Ireland's political, cultural, social, and fashion center.

At 27 years of age I border on being a superannuated student. My rootlessness, my lack of maturity and a certain youthful look, all allow me to blend in. Still, when we gather in the pubs and cheap four-and-six penny lunchrooms of Dublin's South Side, I am often confounded. My compadres punctuate their conversation with nods and winks. Nods and winks are entirely lost on me. And there are customs and conventions of which I am entirely ignorant. There are things that a gentleman simply does not do. Very often I have the nagging feeling that I am doing those very things at that very moment, that I am breaking all the rules. Am I missing something, a shade of meaning, perhaps, or a rainbow of them, a day at the races, maybe? Or a whole raft of horse racing?

The English will forgive you anything, they say, as long as you do it with style. The Irish expect you to know, to be aware, to be in on the joke, whatever the joke may be. "No fools suffered here" could serve as a national motto.

From time to time, in self-defense, during my almost three-year stay in Dublin, I travel down to Limerick City, where I was born, where I grew up, where the ground is less likely to shift under my feet. Usually I stay with the Costelloes. They had been our next-door neighbors, my second family. Sean Costelloe was my surrogate father. When my brothers all left for the United States, Sean became my surrogate older brother as well. His wife, Mary, was sister, friend, and daughter to my mother.

Limerick City, at 120 miles from Dublin, is a three-hour journey by train. I spend a good part of the journey in the bar car. Two small whiskeys, with two bottles of stout singing backup, make for an easy transition.

The train speeds toward Limerick, speeding into memory. Memory, for once, is not receding. Memory waits for me on the station platform in Limerick. I leave the train and walk toward the exit. Trains are diesel now and have been for some years. I feel a foreignness, a layer of awayness, on my skin, but I am reassured by the railway station itself. Walls, rafters, tracks and platforms; all retain their heritage of steam. From this same station we all left Limerick; my mother twice, my three brothers, my father when he took off for England, even my mother's father when he left to join the British Army. We leave. The station waits. When we return, we are embraced and intoxicated by a great breath of pent-up steam.

Eight years have passed since I left Limerick. I expect to go unrecognized, but, on the platform, among porters and baggage handlers, there are a few familiar faces. They nod in my direction. A Limerick nod, by its very nature, bears no commitment, but these are friendly. A returned Yank now, I take a taxi up to Janesboro, to O'Donoghue Avenue, to the Costelloes' house. Sean is out working. Of their children, Jack is living in Dublin. Maria is at work. Gerard is at school. Margaret is with a neighbor.

I was always hungry when I lived in Dublin. Was it lack of flavor or was it the smaller portions? Both, I think. I longed for the diners and the neighborhood coffee shops of New York City, where portions are always generous. I remembered Irish people and English people, coming to New York for the first time and totally taken aback at the volume of food. "Another proof that Americans have no culture," I could hear them think. I smile to myself. In no time at all, I'll bet, they will be diving into the food, just like the rest of us. I had always welcomed the plenty. Plentiful food tells of the gusto, the openness, and the great generosity of the American spirit.

Now, as I knock on the door of the Costelloes' house, it is pelting rain. And I am hungry. Mary greets me, takes my coat, and offers the traditional Saturday lunch: a bowl of packet and tripe. Tripe, the lining of a cow's stomach, is simmered in water for a couple of hours, then cooked with milk and onions. Packet, a kind of pudding, involves a skin casing and the blood from a sheep's stomach. This combination, perfect for a wet winter's day, I demolish in no time. Mary asks, "Would you like a fry?"

"I would."

Now she brings a plate with eggs, sausage, bacon, black pudding, and bread and butter, to be followed by two cups of strong sweet tea. Finished at last, I sit by the fire, at home, and, for the moment, content.

Mary starts to clear the table. Sean arrives. Gifted with a great natural intelligence, now in his middle forties, Sean has always been spare in physique. Despite serious health problems, he cheerfully endures. Done with his morning rounds, in the rain, on his bicycle, he is drenched and hungry. He hangs up his coat, warms his back at the fire, and inquires about the well-being of my family. Rubbing his hands together, he stands in anticipation of the bowl of packet and tripe to come.

When he has finished Mary asks him, as she had asked me, "Would you like a fry?"

Sean is indignant. "A fry? I would not," he says. "Didn't I just have the packet and tripe? What do you think I am, a savage?"

Mary dare not look in my direction. She says nothing. Sean looks at me, then at Mary. He notices the bowl, empty now, which had held my serving of packet and tripe. His glance takes in the egg-stained plate at his elbow and its residue of breadcrumbs, sausage and bacon. Again he looks at me. I am red faced with guilt and riddled with laughter. "By crikey!" he exclaims. Mary gives off a single peal of laughter. Sean smiles. Then he chuckles. "A savage, is it? By crikey, that's a good one." Slapping his thigh, he begins to laugh. Mary bursts into laughter and I just explode.

Saffron

It was late by the time she finished with him and he with her and still no dinner in the offing leading him to intone she offered her honor he honored her offer and all through the night 'twas onner and offer only to receive a playful but very sharp dig in the ribs from his companion as they descended to the kitchen in robes pajamas and slippers

Where she once again dismissed the scandalized servants as he set about preparing the legendary omelet he made only once a year under ordinary circumstances legendary because he put everything into it and always added some spices depending and always on March 18th the Feast of Saint Joseph although why on that day no one knew and he had long forgotten but tradition is tradition

You and your tradition she once said to him you would swear you were Jewish instead of Irish with all this stuff about tradition which led him to protest that you could be Jewish as well as Irish or English or American or Russian or Chinese for that matter or Ugandan and I have never understood why we make that distinction between being Irish and being Jewish when you can be both like Robert Briscoe the former Lord Mayor of Dublin

Good enough said she but distinction or not I am starving now so could you please put your tradition in your pocket and get on with the omelet to which he responded with a righto though in his right mind he would never have subscribed to such an Anglicism but when he was dealing with the omelet he was likely to say anything

As he now assembled a half dozen eggs red green and yellow peppers fried potatoes tomatoes cheddar brie and mozzarella cheese with finely diced apples for the sake of the bowels to which he added a douche of curry or chili for depending on the weather and on his mood he was partial sometimes to the chili at other times to the curry reveling in their attendant aromas as he called them as if the aromas themselves were a line of ladies waiting to satisfy his every whim and not such a bad way to look at an aroma if you are that way inclined and if more people looked at aromas instead of going around with their noses in the air we would have no class warfare and there might be peace in the world as he had been heard to say a sentiment inherited from his own father most likely

Yes he loved chili and curry but saffron he abhorred and to complicate matters he abhorred the word abhorred itself and used it only in extremis claiming that it was nothing short of pretentious in the same league with the word appalling and that no self respecting Irishman would ever use it and that if she should ever find herself in the same room as an Irishman with the word appalling coming out of his mouth she should leave the room forthwith before she became contaminated or worse

For didn't he once utter a loud snort of contempt in a London restaurant when he came across a menu item described as being redolent with saffron which caused him to stand up without warning at the same time ignoring her gently restraining hand on his arm and her
'Alistair, please'
toss his damask napkin on the table and declaim to the dining room at large that saffron gets into every orifice and ultimately clouds the brain to a point at which you are so confused that you wouldn't know whether you are coming or going

Continuing on to say that it wasn't Gandhi who drove the British out of India in all his blessed peaceful resistance and non-cooperation no indeed it was the spice that misted the brains of the poor English causing them to become irresolute muddled befogged and befuddled by an excess of saffron to the point at which the poor buggers didn't stand a chance for the saffron sapped their will and destroyed that famous and admirable English determination

Worse it decimated their renowned ability to muddle through at all costs these the same people who endured the Battle of Britain could not hope to survive such an immersion in saffron for no one not even Perfidious Albion can survive it and she was brought to her knees by insidious saffron he declared

Leading his fellow diners in that London restaurant to sit with their heads down seemingly absorbed in re-reading the menu or scrutinizing the pattern on the tablecloth while across the room a tall distinguished looking gentleman had stood up with a disapproving look as Alistair began his tirade against saffron and remained standing as if in protest but as Alistair reached his peroration the gentleman's expression went from disapproval to puzzlement and now as Alistair reached the end of his remarks the tall gentleman broke into applause calling out heah-heah and applauding even more loudly as the whole dining room joined in

Causing Alistair to pause for a moment nod his head in appreciation and offer a slight bow in acknowledgement which was hardly typical of him and only from the shoulders a man-to-man gesture bearing not a hint of subservience for in all his hardheadedness Alistair had style though never ostentatious he could be counted on to do things right when the time came

Continuing on now as if to exact tribute for his half-bow and to show that he was unbowed he added that if Ireland had had an abundance of saffron the relationship between England and Ireland would have been more clearly defined at a much earlier stage and with a great deal less bloodshed on both sides and then abruptly he sat down as once again the room erupted in a chorus of heah-heah and loud applause

Until the maître d' appeared at Alistair's elbow bearing a silver tray with a note from Management informing Alistair that while he and his party were welcome guests of the establishment for the evening and there would be no bill Management would be much obliged if he and his guests would kindly leave the premises immediately to which Alistair responded by standing once more calling for the attention of the assembled and reading to them the contents of the note

At the end of which there were howls of dismay during which a young man stood up and said
Sir you have offered a great dissertation on the subject of saffron and may I say a thoroughly original analysis of the reasons for our losing

India for which we applauded you though your reference to Ireland and to what was once referred to as 'that damnable Irish question' may have offended some of those present here but still you have been fair-minded in your approach and we of all people respect fairness so I would like to put it to a vote as follows should our learned friend here stay for the duration or not at which there was a loud chorus of yes, yes, yes and the young man said simply the ayes have it

Which brought the maître d' back to the table to discreetly retrieve both note and precious tray on which Alistair had discreetly deposited more than enough cash to cover the bill and to provide for an extravagant gratuity and now having ordered a brandy and port for himself along with after-dinner drinks for his guests and coffee Alistair stood thanked the young man and the whole assembly and paid further tribute to the great English virtues of fairness and fair play

Before launching into a fine rendition of 'I've got a lovely bunch of coconuts' a song beloved of the English working classes and the whole room joined in even the tall distinguished looking gentleman though with a slightly embarrassed air and only at the insistence of the lady to his right presumably his wife though who knows and the evening ended well with expressions of congratulation on both sides along with pledges of peace and friendship

Red Velvet Cake

Even on a rainy Monday, true love is never inert
True love will come with a warm embrace,
to stanch the beloved's tears:
But true, true love's when she alone gets to choose,
the soon-to-be-shared—
Dessert.

Restaurateur

Seeks a safe spot, an oasis, a little island
To be free for a moment from gourmet so grand,
From appetite huge of thrifty gourmand.
He will turn in dismay, from dilettantish hauteur
So consider, ere you speak, your restaurateur.

Ripped Untimely

Carrots taken when they're full grown
(Baby carrots are so delicious)
Apples picked when they're big as a stone
(It really is malicious)
Potatoes dug when they're full size
(When served to us, affront our eyes)

Our taste is urban, sophisticratic,
(Who dares to say we're idiosyncratic?)
We want what we want and we are not agrarian
(Just give us baby fruits and veggies, if need be, by caesarean).

To a Graceless Diner

You've got too much money
And too little brains
Too busy scrounging honey
To come in when it rains
Got your dilled salmon, your creamy brulée
Your briefcase and your suburban sashay.

Got your job and your title,
Gold American Express,
Your private self-indulgence,
massive scorn of public excess.
You'd cream at the sight of Tom Cruise or Tom Hanks
Gurus of your spirit are brokers and banks.

Breeding comes out through the eyes of a cat,
You don't know any better, you forgot to say thanks,
It's too late to learn, what a pity, that's that.

Diet

Fadded and fussed,
Gustatory spirit trussed,
Drank mineral this, ate minimal that,
(One waiter, driven crazy, went in back and ate his hat).

Dieted and measured
Each ingested morsel
Mourned and dearly treasured,
Finally, finally, finally died,
Ordered fresh embalming fluid,
Lite, organic and served on the side.

Monkfish

On West Twenty Seven,
Perhaps a slice of heaven,
In a bistro named Kaspars
Two friar fathers (or is it father friars)
For a tasty but modest and seemly dish
Had shiitakes and greens and roasted monkfish.

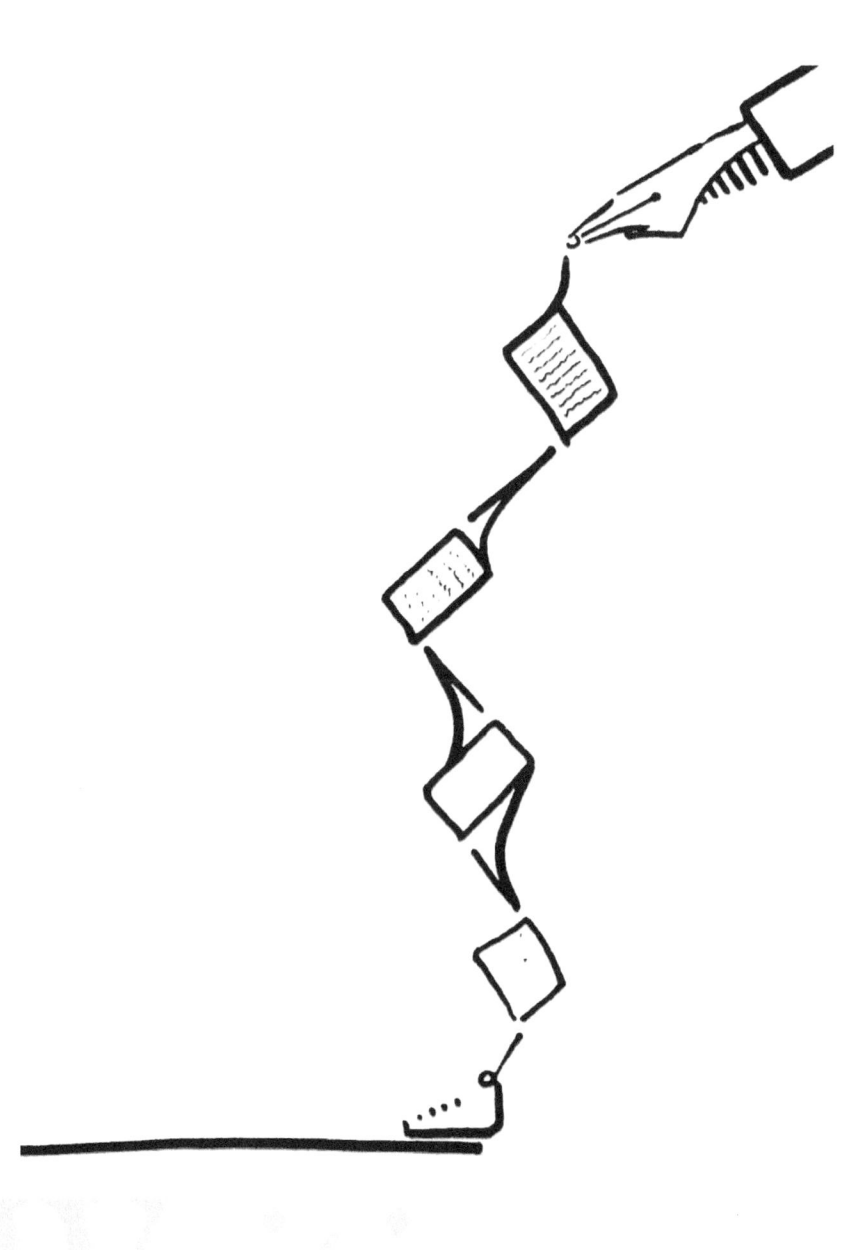

A Poem Is Not a Song

A poem is not a song and neither is a song a poem: so say the wise men, or some of them at least; surveyors, self-appointed, of quantity and quality and I would have to disagree with them, for isn't everything a poem, one way or the other, and isn't there a song in everything?

And isn't every Irishman a poet and aren't we always singing, or so they would have you believe in these here United States of America: but who would ever admit to being a poet, who would own to such a disability, to such an obsession with the architecture and engineering of language, with the search for the soul itself?

And isn't poetry, for us occasional dabblers, but a lasting flirtation with the pretty woman, dark-haired and exotic in a red dress, whom we will never marry for she is not respectable: and we know that if we did marry her, we would be disinherited and the bit of land handed over to the brother who went to America many years ago.

Indeed, and my brother Frank McCourt, though he loved Shakespeare, was fearful of rhyming verse, shell-shocked, maybe, by too much exposure or too great an onslaught of questionable writing shoved under his nose over the years, or maybe he was just leery of rhyme as a suspect currency, as language counterfeit.

For didn't he tell me one time, when we just happened to be talking, "there's no money in poetry": this from a man who spent his adult life working as a teacher, accorded no respect of course and underpaid, who had to wait until he retired to finish the book he had already written seventeen times...

Angela's Ashes, which would turn him into a worldwide celebrity and gain him the worship of millions of women for having elevated one of their own to the status of a heroine: that woman, that heroine, being none other than our mother, Angela...

Whom he portrayed with a light touch as he did our life in all its misery and deprivation, and all the glories of desertion and poverty, with its annals short and simple, he rendered to the music of his pen.

So did this man, so leery of the rhyme, articulate the desperation of our time as children, only to be decried by some and marvelled at with an "oh" and an "oh" again by others, inducing many a "how terrible it must have been" to drown out the mini-chorus of denial.

But Frank allowed no wallowing and no pity, engaged as he was in fending off the solemn on their road to rue, putting begrudgery, in all its grim-faced meanness, in its place: while he painted with humour the four far corners of every auditorium, always with his face toward the light.

Still light on his feet, as he had been when we were young, when Mam admonished us - Malachy, Mike and myself - to be more like him and not to be dragging our feet and killing the heels of our shoes.

Even toward the end when his hearing was completely gone and Lynn, my wife, walked into the hospice room, where Malachy was sitting beside his bed, Frank chuckled, "It was quiet here until you came in!" boasting a broad smile at his own witticism, so casually tossed into the ring of silence, in acknowledgement of his own deafness, oh yes indeed, he kept it light.

And lighter still a few days later when I had made some small adjustment to the sheet around his feet, when once more he beamed, and that was a wrap indeed, when he added, "You're a good kid" ; for soon he would take flight into the great vibration...

Leaving to us the question of poetry, leaving me with a few priceless words, like a piece of verse, a line from a song, or one single painted panel of a series; like my own mental picture of the old men of my childhood when they filled their pipes of tobacco: the warmth of it, the assurance in their measured motions, their quiet murmurings like a musical offering coming just before the ritual lighting up, of the first, soft puff...

... Of smoke, rising, like my memory of a vanished absolute: when there was space for work and room, still, for reflection, before time took us by the balls: when he bowl of a filled pipe still held a small eternity and the flare of a lighted match was cheer enough for now.

And poem enough to light the landscape, a song to shorten the road until the day when "Ah, you're a good kid," Frank's last words to me, would parachute and linger, like the echo of a lifetime.

My Brother Frank:
The Teacher Who Walked Beside Me

My brother, Frank McCourt, died on July 19th 2009: one month, to the day, before his seventy-ninth birthday. The world took notice. Walter Cronkite died on July 17th. My wife, Lynn, said that Frank waited a couple of days so that Walter Cronkite could have his moment. Frank McCourt? And Walter Cronkite, the most trusted man in America at the time? In the same breath? Isn't this a great country!

Frank's early miseries are well known, as are his teaching career, his monumental success as a writer and his vast international popularity as a speaker and humorist. He has always been a strong presence in my life, along with my brothers, Malachy and Michael. I will never speak to him again, nor see him; I can't believe that. But I will have to get used to the idea. Death comes to, and for, everyone.

As is well known, seven children were born to my parents. Three died and, as Malachy has pointed out, for many years the odds were in favour of the survivors. Three were gone and the four of us still stood. Now the odds have shifted.

Frank was ten years older than me, and from my boyhood, I remember him as being serious, austere, even: disciplined, determined and with a sense of mission. Ten years distant from any possibility of an easy relationship with him. I was a little bit intimidated. Until the day I borrowed his bike, crashed it and awaited his wrath. Wrath never came. Frank dismissed the incident without any fuss. In our Limerick, in the bleak harshness of the 1940s and 1950s, no one said 'I love you'. But Frank didn't chide me, or shout or threaten. No, he forbore and, to a child reared on fire and brimstone, more especially on the Irish Catholic version, such forbearance, in the face of destruction and stupidity, was nothing short of love.

In 1949, Frank left Limerick, the city of his rearing, and returned to New York, the city of his birth. We were left behind: Mam, Mike and myself. Malachy was already away in England. Our hearts broke when Frank left.

A long ten years would elapse before I came to New York. And, a couple of years later, in 1961, when I was staying with Frank and his wife in Brooklyn, Frank and I went for a few beers in a bar in Downtown Manhattan. All too soon it is four a.m., closing time, with the dawn coming up; too late and too early to take a subway or bus. At Frank's suggestion, we walk across the Brooklyn Bridge. Two men, walking side by side; fat or thin, tall or small, rich or poor; there's a magic in that.

We are nowhere near drunk. It would be hard to get drunk on even a long succession of small fifteen cent glasses of beer. But we are cheerful. By this time I am as tall as Frank, my oldest brother. Out of the night and into the day we walk, out of the darkness, into the light and the promise of the future. Only in retrospect, and only after many years, did I see the symbolism. To this day I treasure it. Ever the teacher, Frank didn't send me ahead or walk behind me. Nor did he lead. The teacher walked beside me.

Eight or nine years later, when I was living in Dublin and attending University College, Frank came over to work on a doctorate, at Trinity College. I was sharing an apartment with two friends. Frank lived elsewhere, but he had a key to our apartment. One miserable, rainy afternoon I came home to find him in the kitchen. Standing, still in his coat, he was eating a soft-boiled egg. One single, solitary, soft-boiled egg, with no bread, no butter, no tea in sight. That was his way. Only what he needed, that's what he took. He kept the faith.

Twenty-five years later, the success of his first book, a memoir, left him bewildered. Throughout most of his adult life he had been "only the teacher". *Angela's Ashes*, a saga shot through with poverty and hunger, became the engine of his success. Now even *Gourmet* magazine was asking him to write a piece.

"Irony is my constant companion," he would remark, as he poked fun at his status as a newly minted big shot.

Frank survived typhoid fever as a boy and endured chronic conjunctivitis. In the 1980s he would survive cancer. Having thoroughly embraced and enjoyed his dozen years of fame, he was now afflicted with melanoma. Treatments and hospital stays would follow, all to no avail.

During his last days, in the hospice, he lies propped up in bed. Two or three other people are in the room. I indicate to him that I must leave and that I will be back tomorrow. Frank raises his right hand, the first and second fingers extended; the middle finger and the pinkie folded back, the thumb lying flat.

Smiling as he is, this gesture means something, I can tell. The others in the room are watching him and they laugh when he raises his hand. With the crinkle of a joke at the corners of his smile, he forgives the others their laughter. Still looking directly at me, and with the same wide smile, he moves his right hand: upward, and slowly downward, then left to right, in a continuous motion. Oldest to youngest, fatherless now as we have ever been, in timeless rhythm he gives me his blessing. And without a thought, I cross myself.

Next day, Malachy and I are with him in the room. Frank's wife, Ellen, is away, briefly, on an errand. Frank becomes agitated. His shirt is bothering him and we help him to remove it. Still he tosses. We can't settle him, can't seem to relieve his discomfort. We decide to use the emergency device to call the nurse.

"Where is it?" I ask Malachy

"It's hanging by the side of the bed," Malachy answers. I look for it without success, and I continue to search, while Malachy insists. In the end, I get down on my hands and knees. Malachy, with his busted leg encased in the big black boot, begins the search on his side of the bed. Neither of us can find the device.

I have a fleeting vision of Malachy, Mike and myself, all of us under the bed searching for the device, and the nurse arriving in.

"Where is everybody?" she would ask Frank. "Where have your brothers gone?"

"Damned if I know," would be his response. "The behaviour of my brothers has always been a mystery to me." And he would sink back on his pillow, resigned, as always, to our vagaries. That was my imagining. In the event, Malachy's wife, Diana, had gone to summon the nurses.

Frank never had been overweight, and now there is not an ounce of excess. His spirit, whatever that is   his dreamer, his inspiration, the fine tuner of all his lives and of his brilliant articulation, all are pulling way.

He tosses and turns from side to side. No matter how he has been positioned in the bed, his feet always seem to find purchase against the rail at the foot. Now he moves his legs up and down, as if practising for take-off. A distillation is taking place, a fever without fever, as his spirit gains its complete ascendancy. And a smelting, as his body, reduced to its essentials, takes on a sheen and an extraordinary beauty.

Years ago, Frank told me that he was strongly attracted to the writings of J. Krishnamurti; to the idea that we should abandon all the grandiose notions and practices of established religion, that we should look with wonder at whatever is before us, and that, toward everyone and everything, we should behave in a just, loving and compassionate manner. He didn't say this in so many words, but that was the message. Be guided by justice and love. That's the most practical approach.

I hadn't seen or sensed any angels at Frank's bedside. No secular spirit-guides-for-hire, either. I doubt that he would want them. Instead, I believe, he had been getting himself into fighting trim, accepting change as it came, as he always did, shedding all excess baggage and preparing for the trip.

Then the nurses come. With care and tenderness, they move him up the bed, adjust and plump up his pillows and settle him. Soon he is asleep, and he will continue in sleep. There is talk of seizure, of complications. I think I know better. On his left side now and with his left palm under his chin and his chin slightly raised, in the thinker's classic pose, peacefully he sleeps.

Only days later, on Sunday afternoon, family and friends were present at the hospice. I was not. Having stayed with him all night, I was at home when the call came. A little after three p.m. Frank had stopped breathing. His body had finally wound down. It is very sad. The knowledge of his absence is sometimes overwhelming. The memory of that earlier day, that day of exaltation, offers some consolation.

A few years ago he said to me: "We are all we have, the brothers, the women and the children." And now we are one less. Frank should have a nice rest. God knows he deserves it. And maybe, in another sixty-six years, or however long it takes to reach retirement age in the other place, he might just break away from the mass of the great vibration, pay us a brief visit, and, once again, lend his voice to the poor and dispossessed, the shunned and excluded.

Dylan By Two And A Miracle Doubled;
One Man's Village

I live uptown, on the West Side. It was not the Upper West Side when I moved there. That's what it became. There was nothing I could do to stop it. Honest! Powerful forces were arrayed against me; Real estate people, the City of New York itself, the blossoming of Lincoln Center and a certain inevitability. I will go to my grave apologizing for my failure. And I suffer. Only the other morning, as I left my building on my way to work, I had to open the front door for myself. The doorman was not to be seen.

"There's goes the neighborhood," I said to myself. "There is hope for us yet."

Once a week I take a break from the Upper West Side. I drive down to Washington Place to collect my daughter from her music session. Am I the only man in the history of the world ever to go the Village in order to fulfil a duty? Hardly. The Village can be an earnest place. There's NYU. And Bleecker Street is home to the Actors Studio. Nothing is more serious than the Actors Studio.

The Village is often referred to as the West Village. To me it is, simply, The Village. Then there is the East Village, Soho, No Ho, Yo Ho Ho, Tribeca and, of late, Williamsburg in Brooklyn. The Village could be mother and father to them all. That's my view from uptown.

When I first came to New York, from Ireland, I was not shunted off to the ghetto in the Bronx. (That came later). Instead I was privileged to hang out at the bar and in the back room of the Lion's Head under the wing of my brother Frank. There were songs with the Clancy Brothers and with Tommy Makem. Barely off the boat was I when my brothers Frank and Malachy introduced me to the White Horse Tavern. On a solitary pilgrimage of my own I blundered into the Bitter End. A young man on stage sang and intermittently played guitar and mouth organ. Guitar and mouth organ together! It had to be Dylan.

There were parties. The most predictable topic of conversation, exceeded in frequency only by discussion on the care and feeding of cats, was Virginia Woolf and *To the Lighthouse*. I didn't know Virginia Woolf from a bull's foot. Why was she so important? Worlds away, on the Upper East Side, the standard topics were Eugene O'Neill's *Touch of the Poet* and *Under Milk Wood* by Dylan Thomas. I didn't know Eugene O'Neill either, but I knew the legend of Dylan Thomas and his last days at the White Horse Tavern. It seemed as if Woolf and Thomas occupied opposite poles of suicide. She went, sudden and alone, in the water. He went, socially, at least on the surface, over time, in the drink.

To me it was strange. Dylan Thomas had spent his last days in the Village yet his name was most often invoked, not in the Village, but on the other side of uptown. I know now that I could never have risen to Virginia Woolf's level of despair. Dylan Thomas had given his life for his art, using drink as his medium of departure. I could never have aspired to any understanding of him either. But at least I could claim him as a fellow Celt. I could, perhaps, have loped along behind him, at a thousand miles distance and gained a small glimpse of his genius. And when you're twenty, a literary, alcoholic suicide can be a romantic notion. Why then was he not talked about at Village gatherings? Had he been exhausted as a topic? Did he have no cachet or had he suffered the fate of the prophet in his own country?

I could have asked but I didn't. The men bristled with talent. The women, equally talented, large-eyed and lustrous as their long black hair, were far too beautiful and too sophisticated. I was ignorant and intimidated and my timing was poor. Sometimes I formulated something halfway clever and was all ready to say it, only to find that the conversation had moved on. Now they were talking about Dali. Dali??

I learned to hold up my end of a party conversation. It took years. My timing is still more often off than on. But I manage. If you were to believe one of my co-workers, he has to hold me back from talking, not only to strangers in the street, but to the pigeons and squirrels we meet along our way.

Faithful and basically unchanging is the Village. We have a friend, a straight friend. Sometimes, with her bi-friend, she hangs out at a women only bar in the Village. I well remember the man in drag who sat up at a bar in the Village, produced shaving mug, razor and brush, lathered his face and proceeded to shave his moustache. And once, to the Village Gate we went, Leonard Melfi, my wife and I, to see the brothers perform. And we agreed, we three, Lynn, Leonard and me, to a single glass of champagne apiece. Because it was Saint Patrick's Day.

And the Village is constant. Toward the end of last year, on Gansevoort Street, I stand near a playground. Every Wednesday afternoon my daughter goes for a speech class, at YAI, in the building next door and I pick her up, along with Carla, her friend and mentor. On this day in early October the playground, filled with young people of school age, is bursting with the energy of a new school year.

Closed for the filming of a TV commercial, the street is free of traffic. Important people, with badges and radios, shepherd us away from the filmed action and across the street to the opposite sidewalk.

Two young women in their early twenties are the principal players. Fine boned, fashionably dressed and with a purple raincoat over all, the brunette is restrained in manner. She will march only when bidden. Wearing sports clothes and a big smile, the blonde seems more flexible. Sound boom and camera are dominant. We, the adults on the street, crane our necks to see and hear.

Inside the playground there are two young girls. Each holds an end of two ropes. They rotate the ropes, one clockwise, the other counter-clockwise. A third jumps double-dutch. Before each jump she bends, straightens and is ready for the next.

The two principal players in the commercial approach the entrance to the playground.

"Hold it!" says the director.

They halt and wait for ministrations of hair and make up. Two ten-year old boys kick a rubber ball back and forth on the sidewalk and, more than once, into the street. A young man, the traffic warden, with great good humour, kicks it back to them.

A different girl is jumping now. Tireless as the first, she is graceful and disciplined. Freshly made up and newly coifed, the two TV models retrace their steps. Are they Virginia Woolf or Dylan Thomas? Time will tell. And the double-dutchers? They are neither one. They have too much abandon, too much joy. The world will sell its soul for a split-second appearance on television. But these kids have reached a high level of pleasure and a depth of concentration. They are impervious to the camera.

And the Village is always a surprise. On a recent Saturday I went for a walk in the Village. The true geography of Bleecker Street has always been a bit of a mystery to me. On that day I decided to begin at Broadway and to walk west, across and up Bleecker Street. Having crossed Christopher Street, something made me turn right. Coming toward me was a man in his sixties. He had a pronounced limp. Another man came running out of the store a few steps behind the limping man. With his left hand he held a cell phone to his ear. In his right was an object. Had there been a robbery or a theft?

"Sir, Sir," the running man called out.

The limping man stopped. "My God, my cane," he said aloud.

"Man walks away without cane and doesn't even know it," I said to myself. "The first miracle."

Now I walked on, confident of more. A few blocks up was an eating and drinking establishment. The Miracle Bar and Grill. Should I take this to be the second miracle? Maybe. But I had run out of time. This and miracle number three would have to wait for another day.

Curry Egg Salad, Hold the Gleem, Side of Notebook

When Oscar Wilde landed in the U.S. he was asked by a Customs official if he had anything to declare. "Nothing except my genius," declared Oscar Fingal O'Flahertie Wills Wilde. And the official waved him on.

Not so my brother Malachy. About a year after the events of September 11, Malachy was about to board a plane, on his way home from Sacramento to New York.

"Are you carrying any sharp objects?" he was asked at the security checkpoint.

"Nothing but my sharp tongue," was Malachy's response.

"Stand over here," was theirs.

After a very thorough pat down he was allowed to proceed.

A few years ago, Malachy and I, along with our brother Frank, were returning from a short stay in San Francisco. Malachy and I passed through security with no trouble. Not so our brother Frank, the famous one, winner of the Pulitzer Prize, his face well known to millions through his many personal and television appearances. The security agent had a heavy foreign accent. He could easily double for the stereotypical "gentleman of Middle Eastern appearance." He subjected my brother to an extensive pat down, all the while chuckling and chanting, "You are not a good guy, heh-heh-heh, you are not a good guy, heh-heh-heh." It was bizarre.

I was bothered by this behavior but Frank, who had been through a million such checkpoints, was imperturbable. Later on it occurred to us that he had been suspect because of his ticket. Malachy and I had round-trip tickets which covered our flight to San Francisco and back. Frank, having flown from Chicago to San Francisco, had a one-way ticket from

San Francisco to New York. A one-way ticket? A dead giveaway, or so we are told. For the suicide bomber, on a one-way mission, a round-trip ticket is a waste of cash, and Al Qaeda's resources are not what they were.

More recently, as I prepared to board a plane, on my way back from a brief visit to Chicago, I was challenged by security.

"You have toothpaste," the agent said.

"I do," I replied.

"You have toothpaste," she said again.

"I do," I answered, once more.

And again. "You have toothpaste."

I am agreeable, by nature, but this could go on all day and I will miss my plane, so I take the initiative.

"Is there some problem?" I volunteer.

"Yes, you have toothpaste in your bag and the tube is too big."

"Oh," I said.

"Where is it in your bag?" she asks. I move to open the bag. "Don't touch the bag. Don't touch the bag," she admonishes. There is a hint of panic in her voice. "Where is it in the bag?"

"I don't remember."

"Is it at the top or at the bottom?" Thinking that I can speed things up, I move toward the bag. "Don't touch the bag," she warns, once again.

Eventually, the agent follows my directions, negotiates the two zippers, opens the bag, removes the giant, bargain-basement, sale-price tube of toothpaste and, with a most exquisite air of nonchalance, tosses it over her shoulder. I follow the trajectory as it sails in the direction of the giant garbage can behind her. At the moment when it hits bottom, at that precise moment, I will utter a loud "Kaboom." That would be fun.

But I don't. I clamp down on the impulse. Transportation Security Administration personnel are not hired for their sense of humor. Aren't they the ones who make us remove our shoes? And would probably have us remove everything else, as well, if they had their way? Maybe they do have a sense of humor.

I wanted to ask if my toothpaste was destined for testing, later in the day. Would it be the F.B.I.? Or C.S.I. Chicago? Again I kept my mouth shut but I resented the loss of the toothpaste. I had paid good money for it. It was mine. It had been confiscated and tossed. And for no good reason. Would it be sold at auction, given to the poor (I wouldn't mind that), or consigned to some landfill? From time to time I have pined for my orphaned toothpaste.

Then, a few weeks ago, I was returning to New York from a weekend trip to a certain Southern city. The trip, like the other two, was in a good cause. This was a library affair. Our hosts were extraordinarily hospitable, even to the point of providing each of us, the dozen or so participants, with a box lunch to take on the plane. As I approached the security checkpoint with a large carry-on bag hanging from my right shoulder, an old and battered briefcase in my left hand and the box lunch in my right, the security agent offered a cheerful greeting.

"Nice of you to bring lunch," he joked. A joke? From an agent of the Transportation Security Administration? There is hope for us yet.

"Is it O.K. to bring this box lunch through security?" I asked him, as he checked my passport and boarding pass.
"Yes," he said, "as long as there's no liquid in it."

(I was tempted to reward his good humor by presenting him with the box lunch. But I couldn't. To give it away, it seemed to me, would be a violation of the spirit in which it had been given to me and of all the rules of Southern hospitality. I ate it later. The egg salad, with a touch of curry, was delicious).

As I walked through the checkpoint I set off the alarm. In my back pocket I carry a spiral notebook and the spirals are metal. I removed the notebook, placed it in the bowl provided and passed through the detector into freedom. After an hour-and-a-half flight I had to change planes. During the three-hour layover, as I sat by the gate reading a magazine, I felt a nagging sense of something missing, the old and familiar pressure, the bulge of the notebook in my back pocket.

At the airline customer-service desk, I explained my problem. The three people at the desk were nonplussed, as if nothing like this had ever happened before. After much consultation, they directed me to the Transportation Security Administration station.

"Ask for a supervisor," they told me. The lady supervisor at the T.S.A. station was obliging and quickly provided me with a number to call, but it turned out to be a nonworking number.

Some people of my acquaintance will do anything to avoid the direct approach to finding a phone number. They will ask their grandmother, the boy they sat next to in second grade, even the stranger sitting next to them on the subway, almost always to no avail. If I continue to ask around I will be falling into the same trap and I don't have time to fool around. So I call information and I am connected to a woman at the airport of origin. She, in turn, connects me with the T.S.A. station. When I ask the T.S.A. lady if I might have left my notebook in the security area, her answer is cheerful.

"You sure diiyyedd," she chirps. When I ask if they might be able to mail it to me, she passes me to a supervisor.

Again I explain what had happened. The supervisor is sympathetic and she asks if I will be passing through there anytime soon. On a return trip, perhaps? "No, I don't think so," I reply. When I ask if they could mail the notebook, "No, we don't do that," is her response.

But she is, as I said, sympathetic and now, when I tell her that the notebook is of no value to anyone but me, that it contains only random jottings, her tone softens even further.

"Tell you what," she says. "I'll mail it myself, personally." I'm surprised.

"You can do that?" I ask.

"Yes I can."

That was Saturday. On the following Wednesday, the notebook arrives, by mail, all the way, by T.S.A.

(Names of some points of departure and arrival have been omitted, as have names of people involved. All in the interest of security, of course).

The Dry Martini

Literature teems with figures of speech,
Sometimes the allusions are beyond our reach,
Puns well rendered or rendered badly –
We, the reader, must suffer gladly:
Quotes in foreign languages sure cause cerebral friction,
But the very dry martini is still the best American fiction;
The truth, my man, it's gin, straight gin.

The Prose Nose

There once was a man who worked in a bar,
Though he hadn't quite given up on finding his star:
Wrote notes and bits of quotes
On cocktail napkins and on scraps of paper.
They were clever though not profound,
Sometimes he handed them round,
For he enjoyed the caper.

He kept them in his pocket,
Some day to be enshrined in type,
For, secretly, he enjoyed the hype.

Until, one day, came a sneeze incipient,
An almighty sneeze, immediate and urgent.
He plunged in his pocket for a tissue convenient.

Posterity lost.

Well, that's how it goes.
For he stoppered the sneeze
With deathless prose.

Truth

He said, forsooth, in adversity lies truth
For it's hard to see the light
When the sun is shining bright.

But then, said he,
Perhaps you will agree
That verse hortatory
Is a verbal purgatory.

Onion Skin

While all go out to win, win, win,
And the victors give a great shout,
The poet looks up, looks all about,
Finds gossamer gold
In an onion skin.

My Night at Gifford's:
A Dissident Mick Dips Into the Green

It was the twelfth of March, about seven years ago. On the following day, a Thursday, I was to give my annual talk to the women at the Senior Centre, in the Chelsea Housing Co-op where I am employed. At seven o'clock in the evening, the phone rang. It was my nephew, Conor. We said hello – and there was a pause.

"I'm calling for a favour," he said.

I was thinking he was about to ask for help in finding a job or an apartment for someone recently arrived somewhere. I was good at finding jobs and sublets when I was still in the restaurant business.

"You want me to sing?" I joked.

"Something like that," said Conor. "Dad" (that would be my brother, Malachy) "is supposed to receive an award at the City Council tomorrow night. He's out of town and I can't make it and I swore to Brian McCabe that he would show up. I asked Uncle Frank and he can't make it. Can you do it?"

I thought for a minute. Brian McCabe is Conor's friend and colleague in the Police Department.

"What do I have to do?" I asked.

" Just accept the award and say a few words."

" I see," said I.

And I had better see, and clearly, because once a year my wife's employer gives us his tickets to the Philharmonic and Thursday night was the night. I can miss a Broadway musical, with a few exceptions, with little regret. Even the opera I can forego without tears. But the Philharmonic? I crave the Philharmonic. The seats are in the fifth row and center. I listen and watch closely as each musician, each group of musicians, summoned by the conductor, augments the fountain of music. It's wonderful. Lynn was really looking forward to it. And with a day's work ahead, my talk at the Senior Centre scheduled for the late afternoon, and me not yet fully prepared, Thursday would be a full day.

My brothers, Frank and Malachy, are renowned for their public speaking and especially renowned for their humor. They need only stand in front of an audience and people start laughing. Mine would not be an easy assignment. But when would I ever again have an opportunity to say a few words before the City Council of the City of New York? I have lived in New York, more or less, for the past forty years. I have been in City Hall only once and that was for a marriage license.

The family name became well known following the publication of *Angela's Ashes* and other books. I have joined in many 'appearances' and been featured in two documentaries. I still feel, sometimes, like a footnote to the history of my own family. People at events ask me if I am the brother who lives in California. My brother Mike does live in California. God only knows what they ask him. "Are you the Honolulu brother?" maybe or "the brother from Bali?" He doesn't complain, but he once said that given the mortality rate among our siblings and our lack of public credentials, he and I must be 'The Ungrateful Dead'.

Now was my chance. After this one appearance there would be no doubt, not only that I existed, but that I do live in New York. If I never again spoke in public I would have established a definite identity.
"Okay, I'll do it," I told Conor.
"Good. Thank you," he replied, with a degree of relief.
There were no more phone calls. City Hall would be the gathering place. The event would take place at Surrogates Court. Lynn was disappointed at the cancellation of our plans for the Philharmonic, but she was eventually reconciled to the new arrangement which would allow me to stand in the spotlight at City Hall and shed my forty year skin of obscurity.

On Thursday morning I went to work very early and spent time in hasty recapitulation of the material for my upcoming afternoon talk at the Senior Center. The night before, prior to going to bed, I had scribbled a 'few words' to be delivered on Thursday evening…

The afternoon talk went well. The women, and a smattering of men, were generous and spirited. I told them of the bar-room prohibition against discussion of politics or religion, the only two subjects worth discussing. Two very volatile subjects they are, especially among Irishmen. I told them that in a bar, sex could be discussed, but that no man worth his salt talks of his own sexual exploits.

" 'A gentleman never tells' is the adage," I said. They smiled.

"And a gentleman aims for the side of the bowl." The words had popped out of my mouth. They all looked at the floor.

In conclusion, I sang Ed McCurdy's great song, *Last Night I had the Strangest Dream*.

By now it was raining. I was to arrive at City Hall at five thirty. In New York you are early or you are late. You can't be on time. It was still raining at ten after five when I arrived at the security gate.

"Sorry," said the guard, "no-one admitted before five twenty."

"Not even a last minute stand-in for one the three guests of honor?" I could have said. But I didn't. In this climate it is not a good idea to pull rank in the face of security. Ten minutes later, in the middle of a small crowd, I returned to the security gate. Pockets were emptied of spare change and keys and metal objects and I still I managed to set off the alarm,

"Must be the grommets in your hat," said the guard, and waved me on.

Brian McCabe, his wife Jean, and his sister Pat, made me welcome. Their welcome allayed for a while a very personal and very peculiar discomfort which afflicts me when I find myself in a crowd of Irish and Irish Americans. Do I see too much of myself in them, or is it that I have neither a mortgage nor a paid-off house? And I do no charitable work. Will I be found out? Or is it that I see in their faces the mystery of our race and am made wary of it? As, in a wistful moment, my friend Dennis Rice once observed: " Irishmen; always scheming and dreaming." And they are me.

I was introduced to Gifford Miller, the youngest Speaker in the history of the City Council. In the antechamber to his office, to no-one in particular, he sang. He sang the Irish National Anthem. In Gaelic. Remarkable. What will he do for Italian Americans now that he has set a precedent?

There was a photo session with the Speaker. We held up the Proclamations which trumpeted the greatness of my brother and of Mr Gerry Adams, another honoree. (Neither would be appearing). Adrian Flannelly, the third guest of honor, was delayed and we adjourned to the Council Chamber to be formally welcomed by Speaker Gifford Miller. The Chamber of the City Council had become the actual venue. Surrogates Court had been deselected. My first representation there will have to wait until after my death, if, indeed, there is anything left to represent.

Mr Sean Downes, representing Mr Gerry Adams, urged the assembled Council and a full chamber to continue their support of the precarious peace in Northern Ireland. When my turn came, I confided a secret. I said that the real reason for the war on Iraq was not Saddam Hussein's possession of weapons of mass destruction.

"No," I said, "Saddam has a warehouse full of hanging and dimpled chads and if they ever let loose into the atmosphere it will mean the downfall of the Presidency of the United States."

There was scattered applause and laughter; from the Democrats, I imagine.

In the City Council Chamber that night, in the season of Saint Patrick's Day, I wondered, as I do every year, why it is that the Irish Catholics of New York City feel compelled to expropriate Saint Patrick for themselves? Saint Patrick didn't bring Orange Protestantism and militant Catholicism to Ireland. He brought Christianity. Though to hear some people tell it, the snakes he drove out of Ireland were not real snakes at all. Depending on the religious and political persuasion of the teller, the snakes were Catholics lying in wait for the Reformation; or Protestants dreaming forward to the Battle of the Boyne. I think it's a shame that Irish Catholics and Protestants, respectively, cannot give the Pope his due in some other way, on some other day, leave King William of Orange at home and find common ground under the banner of Saint Patrick.

Either way, St Patrick was there, in spirit, in the presentations that followed, to some very worthy people. Among them were the man who devotes his life to bringing disabled young people out of the shadows and into the light; the nun who cares for the children of incarcerated mothers; the man who went, unheralded, every day, to The Site, dodging his way past security, digging and passing buckets with the best.

I had been sitting next to the father of Councilor Christine Quinn. He was full of reminiscence. At the end of the evening the chaplain asked us all to join hands for the Benediction. I reached out to Sean Patrick Sweeney, the intrepid man from 'The Site'. We joined hands. I reached with my left hand toward Mr Quinn.

Under his breath, Mr Quinn said, "This is not us." He had put it in a nutshell. In his dignity and sense of propriety, Mr Quinn is of his generation. He would champion the right and proper and give the back of his hand to the merely appropriate. I sensed what he felt about joining hands. Prayer, even Catholicism itself, was solitary, inward and isolated, when he and I were growing up. Only in the Confessional did we grudgingly open to the pincered probings of the priest as he peeled back the layers of our psyche. Vatican Two was a relief and a diversion, but by that time I was no longer part of the Church.

Sean Patrick Sweeney, a generation behind me, stood balanced on the balls of his feet, ready to march into the jaws of death. Yet he didn't hesitate to join hands in prayer with a man he didn't know. And I, in the middle, between Quinn and Sweeney, reached out to both.

With the Benediction, the ceremonies had come to an end. I shook hands with Mr Quinn and with Mr Sweeney and made my way toward the exit. Two women approached me. The woman to my left gave me a flier which castigated New York City for not allowing an anti-war protest to peacefully assemble, while giving tacit encouragement to a homophobic parade. The flier announced that gays and lesbians would assemble, in protest, on Fifth Avenue, during the Saint Patrick's Day Parade. She asked me to give the flier to my brother Malachy.

The woman on my right declared that she was from County Kerry and had worked in Limerick City (my birthplace) for a Jewish family.

"Finer people you'll never meet," she asserted, as if she expected me to argue the point. "I'm a member of The Ancient Order of Hibernians." (The Hibernians organize the Saint Patrick's Day Parade every year. They fought strenuously to exclude the Irish Gay and Lesbian Organization from marching in the parade).

"I was supposed to get one of them awards myself. A few years ago," she continued. "But I didn't get it." A hint of old skulduggery hung in the air.

Should I introduce the Left to the Right? Each had at least one axe to grind. Better not. Better keep my head. But I can't carry on more than one conversation at a time. So, with an assurance to our lady of the flier that I would pass it on to my brother, I gave my full attention to the AOH woman who had worked for the Jewish family in Limerick. The AOH woman had an advantage. She was accompanied by a beautiful young woman, her daughter-in-law.

"She's from Amsterdam," said the AOH woman.

"No, I am not. I am from The Hague," protested the beauty.

She laughed when I said something about Hagues, Hohenzollerns and Hobokens. But even beauties can have ulterior motives, even those who laugh at my jokes. This beauty gave me a letter from her family and asked me to give it to my brother Frank.

Having gathered up hat, coat, flier, letter and Proclamation, I walked down the marble staircase, toward the main door and the subway. A woman approached me. Fortyish and very attractive, with male escort lurking, she shook hands and introduced herself.

"I enjoyed your joke about the chads," she said.

"Thank you," said I.

"And what's your first name again?"

I told her my name.

"Oh. Are you the one who…?"

"Why not?" I said, before she could finish. I headed for the security gate.

Across the way on Broadway, the pavement was shining. It had stopped raining.

Saint Patrick and the Great Divide

Ireland has produced her share of poets, dramatists, warriors, revolutionaries, novelists, statesmen, and explorers. The Irish are also renowned for drinking, fighting, and singing. And the gods have bestowed on the Irish the most precious gift of all, the ability and the good sense to take everything seriously—and to take nothing seriously. And we do, most of the time. The marching season, the season of the Saint Patrick's Day Parade and the annual confrontation between the parade organizers and the Gay and Lesbian Community, is an exception. This is serious business, with far reaching consequences.

Our new mayor, Bill de Blasio, adds fuel to the fire by declaring that he will boycott the "official" parade on Fifth Avenue on the grounds that the organizers discriminate against certain groups. The mayor (may-will-will not) participate in the Saint Pat's For All parade in Sunnyside, Queens. He is to be commended for doing so. Still, by boycotting one parade and attending the other, he may well exacerbate the tensions between the two groups. And we have a genius for "the split." We've had centuries of practice. Should we look forward to the Parade Committee, the Official Parade Committee, the Provisional Parade Committee, the Real Parade Committee, a plethora of splinter groups—and a similar scenario for the Irish LGBT? The Parade Committee, in this stance, has gone far out on a limb. Let's hope they can find their way back. And the Irish Gay and Lesbian Community should not forget the long tradition which has nurtured the parade: a tradition begun when the Irish, and Irish Catholics in particular, were held, not in low, but in no esteem.

Both sides ought to be wary of even a hint of "Divide and Conquer." The Irish Gay and Lesbian Community, in particular, should not allow themselves to become a political football, a pawn in somebody else's game, especially since the Irish influence in New York City politics appears to be growing less and less. Council Speaker Christine Quinn no longer holds her position. Police Commissioner Ray Kelly has moved on. Our new mayor pushes hard for the inclusion of minorities in city government and the Irish presence is minimal. Our heroic Sanitation Commissioner, John Dougherty, is the only visible standard bearer.

At one time, in the 1980s, the late Cardinal O'Connor announced that he was going on a pilgrimage to Ireland. His good friend, Mayor Edward I. Koch announced that he would go along on the trip. Congressman Charles Rangel, on hearing that the mayor would be leaving town, made only one comment: "New York's gain is Ireland's loss," said Charlie. Mayor de Blasio, the Parade Committee, and the leaders of the Irish Gay and Lesbian Community, could do likewise. They could go on a pilgrimage, a retreat. To the Adirondacks, perhaps. Maybe Whitey Bulger's old gang and the Gambino family can be prevailed upon to provide security. After three days of seclusion, having spent every waking moment together, they will surely work out some kind of compromise. If only to get away from each other.

Ulysses S. Grant, in his memoir, wrote about Georgetown, the village in Ohio where he grew up. Slavery was a major issue. Even in his village of only a thousand people, slavery, and the Civil War, were passionately debated. "There were churches in that part of Ohio," Grant wrote, "where treason was preached regularly, and where, to secure membership, hostility to the government, to the war, and to the liberation of the slaves, was far more essential than a belief in the authenticity or credibility of the Bible. There were men in Georgetown who fulfilled all the requirements for membership in these churches."

Saint Patrick used the shamrock and its three leaves to show that it is possible to have three persons in one God—the Father, the Son and the Holy Ghost. In our time the shamrock is used to mark the location of an Irish bar, a beer, or a toora-loora Irish gift shop. We could restore something of the true meaning of the shamrock, and accord it some dignity by declaring that, given the three leaves, there's room enough for everyone.

We were taught that Saint Patrick brought Christianity to Ireland. Even in Catholic Ireland, where I grew up, there was no mention of

Catholicism in connection with Saint Patrick. Of course Catholicism, as such, didn't exist in the time of Saint Patrick. Still, the Fifth Avenue Saint Patrick's Day Parade is touted as a Catholic parade. The question remains: Is it a Christian parade? Eamon De Valera declared for a Catholic Ireland in the South. Ian Paisley proclaimed that Northern Ireland would remain Protestant. De Valera is gone. In the Republic of Ireland, in the South, the influence of the Catholic Church is on the wane. Ian Paisley and his people are part of the power-sharing agreement in the North. There is hope.

Song: The Immigrant Game

Our grandparents did it they scrubbed and they scoured
Shovelled and tunnelled so we'd be empowered
So we didn't care when the newly arrived
Worked seven days a week well beyond nine to five
We laid on their broad backs the old ethic of work
Tough jobs for small wages – Mick, Mexican Turk
Lowliest labour dishwasher and maid
Like our fanciest neighbour we had servants to trade

We didn't fear change then, things stayed much the same
We could watch at our leisure the old immigrant game

An immigrant nation we were in the past
But this new crop is alien and coming too fast
If we don't watch out now we'll be overrun
And the blame will be all ours when all's said and done
So we've passed legislation to close down the door
On the immigrant nation that we were before
Don't want them sailing past Liberty's lamp
And if we have our way soon we will pull up the ramp

Frightened of change now we want everything the same
No more time or room for the old immigrant game

But we may be in danger of losing our life
Our people's soul suffers desperation and strife
The poor and the rich drift ever further apart
We don't watch out we may need a life raft
Time for a leader to show us the light
Bring us together teach us what's right
Our people's true spirit to be generous still
To welcome the stranger and treat all with good will

No more fear of change now treat everyone the same
Make time and make room for a new immigrant game

Middle America 2000
(The way we thought we were)

We were all well got
No polyglot
Bud and Sue and Mom and Dad
Baseball mitt and fishing pole
Homecoming queen
As beautiful as ever was seen
Lunch-box dad with ranch-style house
Still a dream in his head
With sex still confined to the marriage bed
And heresy the very suggestion of material futility

A vision forever steeped in sepia sunshine
Still the dream endures like half-remembered wine
A happy fool is he
Who treasures such mythology

Now it is the wonder of the age
That such fond yearning gives rise to such rage
That the memory imagined, so serene and idyllic
Spawns division, derision and hate vitriolic.

Lunchers

Our fathers came up from village and hamlet
From townland and shtetl
Our mothers were adept with frying pan and kettle
We make it in business on a bit of college, a hunch
And now look at us
We're out doing lunch.

Quiet Time
(A Manhattan Bar: Afternoon)

Bartender whinnies and stamps like a stallion,
The host with the gray hair traverses the floor,
Busboy, impassive, stands folding napery
Leftover luncher preens like newly washed drapery.

Waiter stares, vacant, at mini-calculator,
While man at front table looks in vain for a waiter,
Habitbound man picks at four o'clock dinner,
Woman, glass empty, would love an encore.

Blonde, frowsy and blowzy, blows smoke in bar corner,
Dust motes and smoke rings catch afternoon sun:
Hotshot young salesman picks nuts like Jack Horner,
Aging go-getter thinks where's all the fun?

The other waitperson for dear life hugs phone,
Cook in the back peers through kitchen porthole,
Man with hand-truck delivery breaks spell with a noise,
And five o'clock crowd strolls in with faux poise.

Owner's not to be found, maybe taking a nap,
Or in the Park, for his mind's sake,
Running an extra lap.

To an Early Morning Brownie

Hail to you o zealous brownie!
Do you live close by or o so far away
As to qualify as an out-of-townie?

At a.m. 7.05, with morning world just barely alive,
In the Seventies near Central Park
(You see so well in the halfway dark)
You ticket for double-parking, side-by-side,
With space to pass about two miles wide.

Do you come in stealth
For the City's fiscal health?
Are you a faithful financial retriever,
Or a vengeful, noxious eager beaver?

You ticket where, minutes, or hours before,
A car window was likely busted.
(Who can be trusted?)
We should be thankful they didn't steal the door.

We know you're for law and all for order,
But of revenues, not thieves, you're a champion warder
(Between you and us citizens the gulf is as great
As old Saddam's ego in invading Kuwait).

We dearly wish that a Saab would rhyme,
Make it easy, do a Ford, or a Chevy, next time.
On second thought, we really should send you flowers
Because, for once… the ticket wasn't ours.

Rasta Danny

Friday, early evening, in Times Square subway station
(When residents have gone away
For one post-summer fling ere sun shall wane)
And only the city's denizens remain,
A rainbow range of every nation;
Finished work is a sweet relief,
The weekend a burgeoning joy,
While a sotto voce saxophone plays a Rasta Danny Boy.

Ireland

Albanese

When Raymond O'Brien left Kilrush he was twenty years old and penniless. Twenty-five years later he returned and proceeded to buy up all the land around his family's two and a half acres. In America he had married Francesca Albanese, thumbed his nose at legalities, custom, and heritage and adopted his wife's family name as his own. "You treated us like dirt. My family was nothin' and had nothin'. Now we'll see how yee'll deal with the Albaneses. Yee'll sing a different song now," he declared, to the four winds and to his neighbors at large, shortly after his return.

Raymond, though a landowner, still lived in the family cottage. In deference to Francesca he had added a second story and an extension. The cottage had been completely renovated to include a modern kitchen, two bedrooms with adjoining bathrooms, a laundry room, and central heating. He turned the cowshed into a guesthouse for Francesca's visiting relatives. Most of his thousand acres he left fallow, under the care of two minimalist, very minimalist, farm laborers. They were not overburdened. His own immediate holding was one hundred acres.

At the far western edge of these hundred acres he built a replica of the cowshed. Raymond himself did the milking. "I like the solitude, the quiet, the rhythm of it. And, milking, morning and evening, keeps me regular," he would say when queried. "It's good for the bowels and it keeps me in touch with me roots." "His roots," the locals mocked, "he wouldn't know a root if he tripped over it though 'tis said his old man had a fine oul bit of a root."

One evening, when he didn't return from the milking at his usual time, Francesca went looking for him. She found him. Sitting on the milking stool, his hands under his chin, elbows on knees, he was gazing into the pail of steaming fresh milk. From the doorway she called his name in the twilight, softly she called to him and advanced into the cowshed. Startled into a hasty return from his far away gazing, he stood up so abruptly, that he almost knocked over the stool.

Seeing but not seeing, sleepwalking almost, he stepped quickly toward Francesca and kissed her. The kiss; lingering and soft, urgent yet restrained, bore the hunger of a lifetime. "Cool. Making you reach and reach, willing yourself to flow out through your lips. Hot. So hot that you wanted his lips on yours till the end of time," she wrote in a letter to her sister the next day. Slowly he lowered her to the concrete floor. Making a pillow of his jacket, he placed it under her. "Oh I longed for it," she wrote. "Never did I think I could want it so much. I'd have given my soul for it."

Stamping and lowing, the cow shifted position, turning her head so that they felt her warm breath. Only a few feet from a small river of slurry, Raymond mounted Francesca, thrust and thrust, pumped and pumped and thrust to bursting. Again the cow shifted position and turned her head away. "A modest cow," thought Raymond. Each time he raised up, just before thrusting, he felt a slap on his trouserless behind. Francesca was sometimes passionate, but this was new. She had never slapped his behind before. Raymond was thrusting faster now and faster came the slaps. "Delicious," thought Raymond. She's really getting into it." The cow was stamping, the tempo of her stamping increasing with each thrust. She had been lowing. Little by little her lowing grew into a blowing and, shortly, to a low bellied bellowing. Raymond, pumping all the way, raced to the summit, shouting, in his triumph; Dalcassians (Claremen), Abu.

They lay back on the straw; Raymond on his back, Francesca nestled against him. Smell of warm fresh milk, smell of cow and slurry and their own sweat, all filled the air. Raymond, in a reverie, was hypnotized by the rhythmic swinging of the cow's tail. Soon a slow smile spread across his face. "It was the cow! It was the cow's tail slapping," he thought. "By crimminny! She's some beauty." And he laughed out loud.

Song: Croppies Come Home

(At the birth of the Celtic Tiger)

We want masons, bricklayers and plumbers galore
There's work for ye now where there was none before
Come home ye fine lads and ye'll stay home this time
For we've missed ye 'tis true beyond reason or rhyme

The call has come over come over
Young croppies come home once again
Come back and ye'll all be in clover
Lots of cash for to keep out the rain

My own father did it in the Seventies, the same
Brought us all back from England to try the same game
But the whole situation lived up to his fears
Though he gave it his best lasted only three years

I've been in New York since the last jobless blight
When they said last man leaving please turn off the light
I'm wondering now should I give it a try
If I do or I don't I'll be sorry by and by

Still the call has come over come over
Young croppies come home once again
Come back and ye'll all be in clover
Lots of cash for to keep out the rain

My wife for the kids' sake says yes we should go
My eldest is ten he says yes he says no
He'd miss all his friends, miss his school and his games
If I uproot him now will I stunt his young fame
If we stay can we bring up the kids the right way
Or will things move so fast that we'll have little say
The two girls are too young and they don't understand
The baby that's coming will choose his own land

Still the call has come over come over
Young croppies come home once again
Come back and ye'll all be in clover
Lots of cash for to keep out the rain

I've done well over here with good work and a house
Could do the same over there if that's what I choose
I can handle bad weather hard work and tough jobs
But how to contend with begrudgers and snobs
When the call first came over I thought it was odd
'Twas for building workers only raised close to the hod
Are the best jobs all gone then and this just a ruse
To get so many back that they'll pick and they'll choose

Still the call has come over come over
Young croppies come home once again
Come back and ye'll all be in clover
Lots of cash for to keep out the rain

Will I go will I say I'll soon make up my mind
But 'twould be a bad joke if we went home to find
That we'd climbed up the ladder right here in New York
Just to stick on the first rung in Leitrim or Cork

Still the call has come over come over
Young croppies come home once again
Come back and ye'll all be in clover
Lots of cash for to keep out the rain

Ode to a Pint of Stout

O pint of stout,
O tower of onyx and ivory:
Majestic you stand,
We turn and sing to dancers,
Dance to singers
Turn again, with the first long pull
And into warmth we enter
Into talkers' mellow harmony:
Now, with the second long draught
We are learning you;
And drinking in adventure's arc,
Sweet promise of romance
Tradition most convivial.

Cobh

Today, I return, for the first time
Not to the place from which I left
But to the place from which I left the place I left,
Like so many, many thousands before me
To our port of tears
Our beloved Cobh.

Diversions

Had our Anglo-Saxon brethren
Eschewed church for something worthwhile
We'd have thought they'd adopted
A thoroughly modern style
But while the Irish may miss Mass
And adjourn to the bars
The English, alas,
Stick to washing their cars.

Danny Private

Long ago we saw Madonna and her young boy toy
And it's long since Sinead tore up the Pope
Is it too much to ask, then, or dare we hope,
That, like certain intimate acts
Which may not be broadcast or faxed,
The singing of Danny Boy
Take place among adults consenting
And only in the privacy of the home.

Silent Night
And Frank Won't Be Calling This Year

H. L. Mencken described a bar in a poor neighbourhood as 'a clean and well-lighted place'. For us, on Christmas morning, the church was all of that, and more. My father was forever gone and my two oldest brothers, Frank and Malachy, would soon emigrate. My brother Mike would leave when I was fourteen. In memory, and to this day, the Christmas season in general brings on a yearning. But Christmas Eve? Christmas Eve was, and still is, the best part of Christmas.

Tommy Drennan, our local-hero boy soprano, soared beyond heaven when he sang O *Holy Night* at Midnight Mass on Christmas Eve. I will hear him when I am older. For now, at age eight, just past the age of First Communion, my pals and I are too young for Midnight Mass. O *Holy Night* and Midnight Mass are for the grown-ups. We are shut out but we find a way to mark our Christmas. Like fugitives, with only tacit permission from parents and elders, at four a.m. we rise up out of muck and misery, bid so long to the fleas, and , in the blackness of the December morning, hike on up to the Redemptorist Church. This is the Church of Saint Alphonsus. I can feel at home here for isn't the church named after me, or so I tell my friends. And we laugh in the fugitive dark.

At this time of year, the stars hang low in the sky. We pretend to follow one, as the Three Wise Men are said to have done, and allow it to lead us to the earliest Mass, the five a.m.

After the crowd and the riot of music attendant upon the midnight Mass, the five o'clock Mass bestows its own serenity. Even the priest, in his short sermon, offers no rebuke for our burgeoning sins, spares us the customary castigation and delivers the simple Christmas message of Peace on Earth to Men of Good Will. Among the sparse congregation of oldsters, sleepless in their piety, and us few younger ones, with our own brand of sleeplessness brought on by excitement and by the freedom of our dawn-breaking escapade, the message is readily embraced.

At compulsory Mass on a Sunday, we waited impatiently to be released. When the priest intoned the *Ita Missa Est*, the 'Go, the Mass is ended', we answered most cheerfully, with 'Thanks be to God'. Now, on Christmas morning, we are sorry to leave the warm, brightly-lit church and head on home to the snoring indifference of our elders. I will stay outside as long as I can, then go inside and try to amuse myself, without making any noise, while I wait for Mam to wake up. Maybe there will be something special for breakfast, something other than bread and tea.

That's as much as I can remember, or maybe as much as I want to remember, of the Christmases of my childhood. It may be as well for aren't we the only family in history ever to have had pig's head for Christmas dinner, as chronicled by my brother Frank McCourt in his Pulitzer Prize-winning memoir, *Angela's Ashes*, although I don't remember that particular dinner either. I must have been too young.

When we first came to New York, my brothers Frank and Malachy and Mike did their best to create a family Christmas – with mixed results. We did gather for Christmas, all of us, or some of us. But, somehow, someone would always arrive very late, or a little drunk, or with a partner who didn't fit in. I don't know about other families, but our expectations, after so many miserable Christmases, were very high. At least, mine were. Still, even with my own exalted expectations, I was sometimes the offender against the ideal. But the gatherings worked out – more or less.

Until one Christmas dinner in Brooklyn, hosted by Frank and his first wife, Alberta, which went in seventeen different directions. Someone said something. Someone else was offended. A guest fell down the stairs, was not injured but still managed to have a fit and, as I have often been reminded, I threw a paper cup across the room, at no one in particular, and then declared, "I hate violence."

My mother's friend, Violet, was from Europe. She sat in her black dress and black Oxford shoes, in silence and a state of complete bewilderment. Finally she made her pronouncement: "Ve never do these things in Switzerland." And the party ended. It all happened because the turkey was very late in emerging from the oven. One wag observed that the turkey stuck his head out, took one look around and slid back into the oven. He felt safer there.

That dinner has become part of the family lore. We often laughed about it. In the beginning I had a nagging feeling that maybe we shouldn't be laughing, that we should do better at Christmas. It would take me many years to realize that the ideal, or the idealized Christmas, is all too often framed in someone else's window.

Frank left Brooklyn a good many years ago. At the peak of his popularity, which was brought on by the phenomenal success of *Angela's Ashes*, Frank derided his own celebrity. "Mick of the Month," he would say. "That's what I am." And later, "I'm a Mega-Mick."

During his last illness, when he was in hospital, he was stoic. His only complaint was that he was in the *wrong* hospital, that over in the *other* place, the big cancer hospital, they paid attention to celebrities and that he was not getting his due. And then he laughed.

December 21st 2009 marked fifty years since he met me off the boat and brought me over to Malachy's apartment. He died in July of 2009. I saw him only occasionally during the dozen years which elapsed since the publication of what I have come to call A.A. His celebrity took him all over the world. During the years preceding his celebrity, when he was "only the teacher", as he described it, he used to say that he wanted to mingle with powerful men and beautiful women. He certainly got his wish. Even so, even when he was travelling, he always called on us on important days, Christmas being one of them. In 2009, he took the final trip.

He had always been there, our Frank, but not now. And he won't be calling any more. Powerful men everywhere will miss him. So will the beautiful women. And so shall I. I am tempted, almost, to rustle up a pig's head and serve it for Christmas dinner, in memory of him. But

I never did like pig's head, a local delicacy in our Limerick. And some people might be offended. Besides, what would I use for stuffing?

Anyway, he hardly needs a commemorative pig's head. There were a number of memorials, most notably the one for family and close friends, about two hundred of us, at which former President Bill Clinton spoke with eloquence, warmth and humour. When someone organized a Month's Mind Mass for him up on the West Side, Father Brian Jordan, the celebrant, welcomed all of us to the church, saints and sinners alike, and gave out Communion. When I told him I hadn't been to Confession in a hundred years, he gave me absolution there and then. He was kind as the priest had been on that long ago Christmas Eve. I am almost tempted to go back for more. Almost.

And there may well be a few more such occasions. But maybe by another anniversary of his death, they will come to an end and Frank will be able to get some rest. About ten years ago, we were talking about death, burial and cremation.

"I won't be buried at all, or cremated," he said, "I'm going to be stuffed and mounted."

After all this time he must be tired of standing on tiptoe in hopes of catching a glimpse of the speaker and maybe an echo of what is being said about him. Let him sit down, now, and let him take his ease.

And have a good Christmas, wherever he may be.

Allison's Song

They don't know how to see me
They don't know how to look
I don't fit in any category
Don't appear in any textbook
It was alright when I was a child
If I acted up they said I was just wild
Later they said little girl so pretty
Later still they said oh what a pity

And I felt the way they looked at me
So I looked away instead
And a teardrop touched my shoulder
 Just as I turned my head

We'd go to the diner when I was a kid
And I'd hear the waitresses say
Don't worry about her no matter what I did
Got one just like her at home or away
Used to be that my world was round
Warm and bright full of musical sound
Now it's turning flat and bleak
How I wish I could clearly speak

And I felt the way they looked at me
So I looked away instead
And a teardrop touched my shoulder
 Just as I turned my head

It was ok while I was in school
There was a daily place for me
Now at twenty-one I feel a bit of a fool
Because they tell me that I am free
Question is if I'm so free
What's to become of me
Dayhab, Rehab to a group home

Or to an institution so far way from home
And I felt the way they looked at me
So I looked away instead
And a teardrop touched my shoulder
Just as I turned my head

My speech it is there but it's not very clear
Behaviour sometimes off the wall
They tell me I really have nothing to fear
But I'm afraid I might just take a fall
I don't look too different but I sound a little
To look at me you'd never know
That I'm not the person that I could be
That I still have a long way to go

And I felt the way they looked at me
So I looked away instead
And a teardrop touched my shoulder
Just as I turned my head

For now that's my story
But you shouldn't worry
I know that I'll be just fine
Just keep in mind I'm aware and I care
I just walk on a different line
My future can't lie in a shut-in program
Got to be like any woman or man
Do my share in the world we all live in
As a fully-fledged person…I can yes I will
Yes I can yes I will yes I can

I still feel the way they look at me
I still look away instead
But no more teardrops touch my shoulder
Though I still turn my head
No more teardrops touch my shoulder
Though I still turn my head

Lynnie's Song

We said we would leave it to time
Life doesn't give any reason or rhyme
Surely we would meet again
Along the river or out on the plain
Sure as morning brings daylight
Through the miles through the years
We would never lose sight
We'd keep faith and it would bring us through
You to me – and me to you

'Twould be like heaven almost heaven
Perfect blend light colour and sound
Perfect end and a new beginning
Life made sweet complete and round

With you alone I yearn to go
To a place where sparkle rivers flow
Endless miles of windswayed wheat
Where land and deep blue sky do meet
And in a noontime sungold glowing
Touch balming fingers to your tender soul
By cool pendant moon in a field of stars
To kiss to heal your psychic scars

'Twould be like heaven almost heaven
Perfect blend light colour and sound
Perfect end and a new beginning
Life made sweet complete and round

Green and yellow gold and blue
Health and friendship and riches too
Harmony and love forever joined
You and I in body and mind
You and I in body and mind

January 1985

Andersontown,
Belfast, at twilight time
My father has just died:
Fumes and coal smoke ascending
Palls of grayblack under cloud
Create a most repressive shroud.

No clearing here,
No plume of white,
No pope elected,
Precious little hope,
Not even here
In Roman Catholic
Andersontown.

Family

You can choose your friends
But not your family
Not even current trends
Can supplant sibling rivalry.
You can't choose them
That's all too true
But if it's any consolation
Neither can they choose you.

Frankie Came Home
(At the time of the Doctorate)

Frankie McCourt came home.
He did, so he did
Home to Limerick
For his Honorary Doctorate of Letters
At the University of Limerick, no less
And his brothers Malachy, Michael and Alphie
To sing backup and lend moral support
To rejoice with their brother and to honor him
And their American wives came
Ellen, Diana, Joan and Lynn

Seemed all the University turned out
Resplendent-Frank in cap and gown
Emotional, eloquent, overjoyed –
With echoes of Johnny Mac come in for your blue duck egg
That no one else in the lane has
Tommy O' come in for your castle o' pandy

And drinks later and in the evening a splendid dinner with
Speeches of congratulation and acceptance
And then the songs, the songs –
From Eileen Aroon to Broadway
When Mary Costelloe sang 'My Lagan Love'
All the memories flooded in
And made us hunger again

And that night the stranger passing by what's left of the lanes
Below Barrington Street and up in Barrack Hill
Was not at all surprised to hear
Frankie come in, Frankie McCourt come in
Come in for your Doctorate of Letters
This minute.
Come in.

A Song For Our Times

There's something about you
Reminds me of me
If I could just drink you
We'd be my cup of tea

Love and To Be

Love we learn from our fathers
Love in a soon and someday perfect world:
Our women teach us just to brave it
Whatever we are to be.

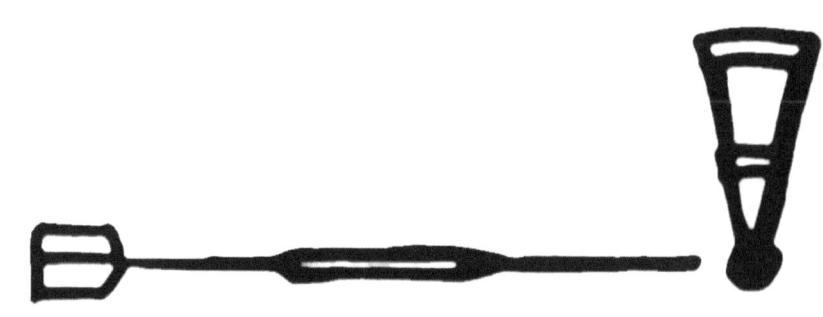

You Don't Say

Paranoia

If paranoia is its own reward
Then perspective is its own prison.

Greed

'Taint the needy that's greedy.

Age

Age is but a shortening of the neck
With a consequent loss of flexibility
And perspective.

Angst

Angst creeps in
Like arthritis of the mind
The moment we begin
To fail to see the point.

Cachet

The ill conceived, ill equipped, climb to cachet
Only results in mundane cliché.

Life

Mosquito thrives on the stagnant pond:
Terror feeds on hunger's cry.

Acknowledgements

Dominic Taylor at Revival Press published much of this material under the title *Heartscald*. My thanks to him for doing so and many thanks for facilitating publication of this expanded collection. My thanks and deep appreciation go to Fiona Clarke Echlin who did a superb job of editing *Heartscald*. A sincere thank you to Ronan Deevy for the illustrations in *Heartscald*, some of which are used in this collection. A special thank you to Dania Fernandez Fernandez for the *Heartscald* book design, some of which is being used in this current collection. And for the cover design, which is being used as the cover of *The Soulswimmer*.

Marta Szabo was kind enough to introduce me to Brent Robison. Brent provided a road map to publication, answered a million questions along the way, gave me the benefit of all his knowledge, wisdom and experience, and brought *The Soulswimmer* to a satisfying and successful landing. Joe Tantillo augmented the original book design to accommodate the new material and is deserving of my sincere thanks..